SOCIETY IN ACTION

PETER & JOAN MOSS

Oxford University Press 1988

Contents

Acknowledgements

The publisher would like to thank the following for permission to
use photographs:

Age Concern: 15C
ASH: 33
Barnaby's Picture Library: 22, 29C, 88T, 107, 137, 147T & BR, 153
BBC Hulton Picture Library: 21B, 23TL
Format Photographers: 26 (Maggie Murray), 57B (Jenny Matthews),
108CL (Joanne O'Brien)
Fotomas Index: 102TL
Friends of the Earth: 108BR
John Frost Historical Newspapers: 102BL (Daily Mail)
Sally and Richard Greenhill: 6R, 7, 14, 21T, 23B, 30, 31TL & BL,
43TL, BL & BR, 55, 102TR, 108TL & BL, 121
Independent Broadcasting Authority: 99
Inner London Probation Service: 88B
Department of Medical Illustration, John Radcliffe Hospital, Oxford: 6L
Mansell Collection: 40
MENCAP: 43TR
Moss Photo Library: 149TL & BR
Department for National Savings: 81L
Network Photographers: 31TR (Laurie Sparham), 34B (John Sturrock),
57T (Steve Benbow), 95 (Chris Davies), 122T (Katalin Arkell), 127B
(John Sturrock)
Oxfam: 146L (Mike Goldwater), 146R & 147BL (Jeremy Hartley)
Popperfoto: 75, 108TR, 115
Rex Features: 23TR, 29L & R, 31BR, 34T, 49, 51, 70, 71, 81R, 102BR,
113, 122B, 148, 150
Save the Children: 149B (Penny Tweedie)
TUC: 127T (Ken Randall)
Women's Royal Voluntary Service: 15T & B

Designed and illustrated by Ray Fishwick

Oxford University Press, Walton Street, Oxford OX2 6DP

Oxford New York Toronto
Delhi Bombay Calcutta Madras Karachi
Petaling Jaya Singapore Hong Kong Tokyo
Nairobi Dar es Salaam Cape Town
Melbourne Auckland

and associated companies in
Beirut Ibadan Nicosia

Oxford is a trade mark of Oxford University Press

© Oxford University Press 1988

ISBN 0 19 833528 8

Typesetting by Typestylers Ltd, Ipswich, Suffolk
Printed by Butler and Tanner Ltd, Frome, Somerset

The family and the individual

SOCIALISATION

Children left to grow up without any guidance or correction would become totally selfish, uncontrolled adults without any consideration for anyone else. Society tries to make people behave in ways which will allow them to live in a community with as few problems as possible, for the benefit of everyone. This is called *socialisation,* but, of course, it does not always succeed completely or there would be no disputes, no quarrels and no police.

School. School reinforces much of the home training, and adds new elements such as working together, playing fairly, being punctual, sharing, working hard, and paying attention. Schools often give religious training in the widest sense — understanding, forgiveness, toleration of others' views.

The neighbourhood. Local inhabitants can bring pressures on people to conform to what that society needs. They can show disapproval of anti-social behaviour such as drunkenness, untidiness, and vandalism.

The media. The press, TV and radio are powerful influences in showing what society expects from its members and by reporting what happens to those who disregard the rules. ('Crime does not pay'.)

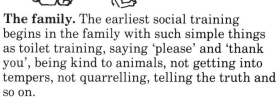

The family. The earliest social training begins in the family with such simple things as toilet training, saying 'please' and 'thank you', being kind to animals, not getting into tempers, not quarrelling, telling the truth and so on.

Peers. Friends of the same age help in social training by demanding loyalty, unselfishness, group discipline and conformity. Peer groups of the wrong sort (gangs) can, of course, be an influence for anti-social behaviour, such as hooliganism.

Work. Work and work colleagues can enforce such qualities as punctuality, doing a fair share of the job and not scrounging, honesty and cooperation.

The law. The law, the police, the courts and prisons exist to enforce the rules of society and to punish those who do not obey them. One of the main functions of government is to make laws which are for the good of the community as a whole.

CHILD DEVELOPMENT 0 - 5 YEARS

In the first five years a human being learns far, far more than it does in any five — or even ten — years later in life. From a totally helpless, totally dependent creature at birth, it becomes an active individual at five, capable of walking, talking and taking a definite part in the world around it.

But this incredible development begins long before birth. At the very roots, of course, much depends on the combination of genes at fertilisation — a process over which no-one has any control. In the next nine months however the mother especially can contribute considerably to what her child will eventually be.

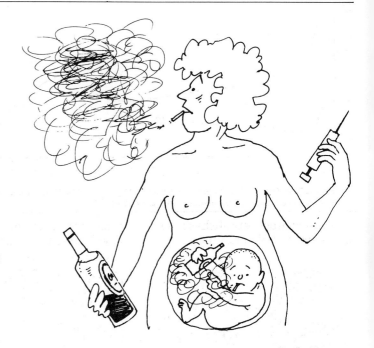

It is now recognised that heavy smoking, drinking or drug-taking during pregnancy can have a very serious effect on the unborn child: smoking can result in low birth-weight and low intelligence; alcohol in mental retardation; and drugs in withdrawal symptoms. What the mother takes into her system must be absorbed by the embryo.

Yet even with the greatest care things may go wrong with the foetus, but today many of these can be detected by ultra-sonic scans (repeated X-rays may damage the embryo) or by 'amniocentesis'. This is the laboratory examination of a sample of the fluid surrounding the embryo in the uterus. It can show that the child will suffer from Downes syndrome (mongolism) or a number of very serious conditions such as spina bifida when it is born. If these are detected the mother will be given the option of abortion.

Children's development is very variable, and has little to do with intelligence. Some attempt to walk at 10 months while others who have had equal encouragement are still not doing so at 18 months. Some say their first words well before their first birthday: others are still babbling at two, though they may be understanding a great deal of what is being said to them. These differences are most noticeable in the first three years of life when development is so rapid and so marked.

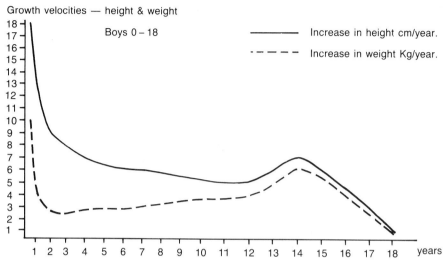

Growth velocities — height & weight

Boys 0 – 18

——— Increase in height cm/year.
– – – Increase in weight Kg/year.

years

These graphs show that the greatest increase in height and weight take place in the first two years. There is another spurt between the age of 12 and 14.

Development in physical, mental, and emotional areas is not steady, but goes forward in spurts. A child will grow rapidly for a month or two, and then not grow at all for a similar period. It may speak one or two words, and then frustrate its parents by not adding another for many weeks. This seems to be a natural process, but progress in the mental and emotional fields can be helped, or hindered, by the environment in which the child grows up. These are some aspects which can play a part in shaping the future adult.

Physical contact establishes a bond and seems to help stability.

Talking to and playing with a small baby even long before it can understand seems to stimulate development. Rhymes and nursery songs are also important.

Understanding natural development and not trying to force — or ignore — it.

Not giving too much or too little freedom — encouraging independence while not depriving the child of the security it needs.

Introducing the child to a wider circle of both adults and children when it is ready.

A violent and fearful home atmosphere will have adverse effects even before the baby can understand what they mean. Love and affection have very beneficial effects.

7

MARRIAGE

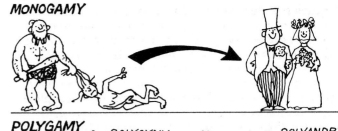

Many people say that marriage is most like a trap — those outside cannot wait to get in to get at the bait, and those inside cannot wait to get out because they realise what it is! Yet in spite of this the population of Britain over the age of 16 is divided up as shown in the diagram below.

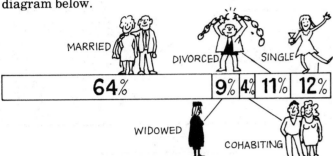

Marriage in one form or another seems to have existed since the very beginning of the human race, so that it must have some important functions. Generally marriage has been monogamy (one man and one woman) but in some cultures there has been polygyny (one man having several wives) or polyandry (one woman having several husbands).

Functions of marriage

Marriage helps to make society stable. (1) Married couples tend to settle down and work to maintain themselves and their home. They have responsibilities to the community so that they are generally law-abiding. (2) They have mutual affection and support so that there are fewer quarrels with outsiders, and fewer problems of disputes over the opposite sex. (3) Marriage often leads to children — and even more stability. The married couple are largely responsible for the social and emotional development of their children, and the creation of the next generation of adults. (4) Married couples can play a large part in the care of elderly, sick or handicapped relatives of both spouses. Today the state has taken over many of these responsibilities, but the family still has a major part to play.

Cohabitation

Today many couples (10-12% of the population over 16) live together in permanent or semi-permanent relationships without being formally married. Because of the tax laws in Britain this relationship can offer financial advantages. It also saves the cost and stress of divorce if the couple decide to separate. Because the couple are not tied by any legal bonds they often have to try harder to keep their partner. But there is a complete lack of security, especially for women as they grow older, or if there are children. Many couples feel a need for some formal marriage after a number of years of cohabitation, especially if they want families.

Perhaps a perfect partner for every person exists somewhere, but in the 20-29 age group alone, where most marriages take place, there are in Britain about 4 million males and 4 million females. In theory there are therefore 16 000 000 000 000 possible combinations. The odds against finding just the right partner seems impossible, yet the majority of people do make satisfactory marriages because in most cases there is a 'filtering' process which eliminates all but a few candidates.

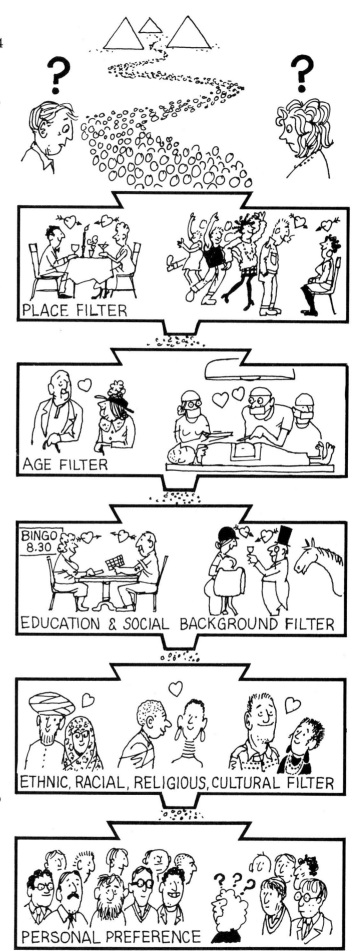

Place. The majority of people marry someone from their own district. This is natural because they have a good chance of meeting at school, at work or at local entertainments, and getting to know each other well. Today, with more mobility, more people are meeting others from different parts of the country, or the world.

Age. Most marriages are made between people whose ages are within 5 years of one another. This is natural because people of the same age are most likely to have similar interests, and meet at work or at entertainments. There is a tendency for the male generally to be a few years older — average age at first marriage in Britain is 25 for men and 23 for women.

Education and social background. In a majority of cases the couple have similar educational and social backgrounds because their interests and attitudes are more likely to have common ground. The theme of the 'prince and the showgirl' is more common in stories than in real life.

Ethnic/racial/religious and cultural. Although the position may change in the next generations, today most people chose a partner from their own ethnic, racial, or religious group. This may be more because of family pressures than personal preferences or because they meet more of their own group than outsiders.

Personal preference. Some or all of the factors above may eliminate the vast majority of possible partners, so that people are generally left with a manageable number out of the 4 million. Then personal preference makes a final choice — physical appearance, personality, similarity of interests and attitudes, sheer accident — and love.

There are, of course, many successful marriages which do not conform to these patterns — widely different ages, completely different social, educational or cultural backgrounds.

DIVORCE

Until 1857 divorce in England and Wales could be obtained only by a special Act of Parliament. At today's prices it could cost tens of thousands of pounds. It was so difficult that in 300 years only about 150 divorces were granted. Even after 1857 divorce was still not easy, and in 1901 there were only 848.

After World War II the divorce laws were steadily relaxed: in 1961, 29 000 marriages were dissolved (3 per thousand married couples in the country); in 1971, 75 000 (6 per thousand); and in 1984, 158 000 (12 per thousand). Today, one in every three marriages will probably end in divorce.

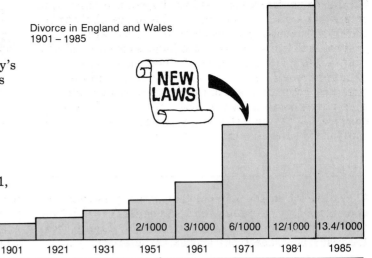

Divorce in England and Wales
1901 – 1985

NEW LAWS

1901	1921	1931	1951	1961	1971	1981	1985
			2/1000	3/1000	6/1000	12/1000	13.4/1000

Reasons for increased divorce rate

New laws have made divorce easier and cheaper and one unwilling partner can no longer block a divorce.

It is easier for a woman to support herself financially today — she is not so dependent on her husband for money. 72% of divorces are granted to women.

Longer expectation of life. 150 years ago a typical marriage lasted about 15 years before the death of one partner: now it is over 50 if there is no divorce. What people can stand for 15 years they may not for 50!

Rise in divorces
Undefended cases heard at Divorce County Courts. Defended cases heard at High Court in London.

Marriage partners have more freedom outside the home and are more likely to meet other people they prefer to their spouses.

Social attitudes have changed — divorce is no longer looked on as a crime. In the past even the 'innocent' party was often regarded as having been disgraced.

The older complicated system of grounds for divorce — adultery, cruelty, desertion etc — has been reduced to one: 'irretrievable breakdown of marriage'.

Effects of divorce

On money/property. The division of money, property, and possessions when a marriage breaks down can be settled informally by the two people concerned, or a judge may be asked to sort out the matter. The husband is compelled to provide for his ex-wife and children (the law also allows in special cases the wife to maintain an ex-husband), and if necessary the court can order the money to be taken directly from his wages. The maintenance order remains until one party or the other applies to the court to change it — a man whose ex-wife was living with another man could ask for his maintenance to be reduced or abolished.

On children. Many spouses in a divorce are relieved to be free of each other, but their children are likely to be emotionally upset. The problems of custody are generally settled in court — the judge's concern being what is best for the children. He has to assess the situation in each case, and normally small children would be left in the care of the mother, though this need not be necessarily the case. The judge will also decide when the parent who has not been given custody can see the children, and for how long.

One-parent families. One family in every 14 consists of a single parent living alone with dependent children. 88% are mothers, 12% fathers. One-parent families are the result of (1) death of a spouse, (2) desertion by a partner, (3) divorce, (4) unmarried mothers who are unwilling or unable to live with the father. However good the single parent might be there can be problems which a typical two-parent family does not have to face.

Missing parent. Although many single parents make an excellent job of bringing up their children they are often handicapped by lack of money and tiredness in trying to take on both roles and work at the same time. It seems natural for children to need both parents, and they may suffer emotionally from having only one. Some parents may over-compensate and spoil their children: others may under-compensate and be harsh, and often bitter against the opposite sex.

Financial. It is often difficult to trace fathers who should be supporting their children. It is also difficult for mothers, especially with small children, to find suitable work. The shortage of money makes finding decent homes a problem. The government does give extra social benefits to one-parent families, but this is not nearly as much as should be provided by the missing partner.

Reconciliation — marriage guidance councils. Marriage guidance councils are voluntary organisations of trained counsellors to which couples who are having problems with their marriage may go for help. The aim of the counsellors is not to give advice, but to get the couples to see their own problems and possible ways of solving them. The aim of such councils is to prevent the breakup of marriages, and to encourage reconciliation.

Conciliation. Some probation officers are specially trained in matrimonial difficulties. A court may suggest that a couple who are being divorced and have children should consult the conciliation officers. Their job is not to try for reconciliation, but to try to make the process of divorce less bitter, especially with regard to the custody of the children.

THE FAMILY

What exactly is 'a family'? Is it a man and woman, either formally married or as partners, living together in a joint home, sharing costs and work together?

Is it a man and woman and their own children? When these are born are other relatives more or less excluded from 'the family'?

Is it the man and woman together with their relatives? If so, how far do the relatives extend? Parents? Brothers and sisters? Grandparents? Uncles and aunts? Cousins?

Whatever we may think of our family — parents and relatives — we normally have to accept them for at least the first 16-20 years of our lives. We are tied to them by heredity — we tend to look like them and have similar personalities (though these may be through training rather than genetic make-up). We generally have deep bonds of affection, and sometimes duty. They have contributed largely to the way we behave and our whole attitude to life. And on a practical level we are tied to them for economic reasons — they support us, provide us with food and lodging and generally look after us. Sociologists divide families into two types: 'extended' and 'nuclear'.

The extended family. This is the older type of family where the couple and all of their relatives tend to live near one another in the same village or town. Sometimes though not very often, several generations live in the same house. Until the industrial revolution in the 19th century it was generally difficult for most people to move from their home district because of the problems of finding work, and limited transport. For some time after the industrial revolution members of the larger family tended to live within a short distance of one another because many of them worked at the same factory or mine. Extended families are found in the older industrial areas of Britain.

The nuclear family. This consists of a couple and their children alone, with the rest of their relatives living a long distance away. With the industrial revolution there were more jobs available all over the country and people moved to find better work and promotion. This was made easier by improved transport. They settled down in homes of their own in new towns where they knew no-one, with parents and children forming a nucleus. Naturally they soon made friends but these people they could choose for themselves, and they were usually of their own age and with their own interests and outlook. In the extended family they had little choice — there was a built-in circle of their own relatives of all ages and strong pressure to conform to the 'family' ideas.

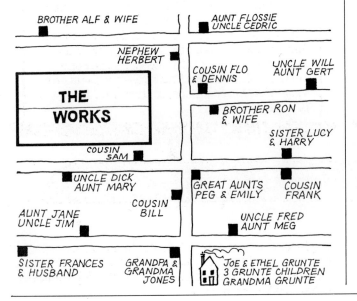

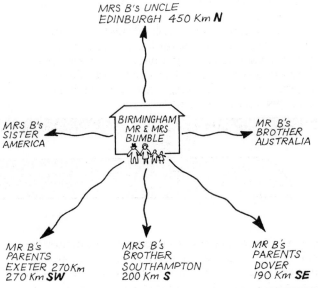

Nuclear vs extended families

In an extended family there is always a relative near at hand in times of trouble, death, or to look after children or the elderly. Grandparents especially can teach children old skills and crafts, tell them old stories, and play a large part in early education. Constantly meeting other relatives can establish a strong family feeling.

There is a greater chance of quarrels, especially between younger and older members over the younger generation's behaviour and ideas. There can be divided loyalties between husband and wife over their own families. Children can be spoiled by other members of the family, especially grandparents, and their own parents' authority undermined. Outdated traditions, attitudes and prejudices can be passed on.

Nuclear families can often be lonely, especially in trouble or illness, when friends may not be so friendly. They have to rely on impersonal organisations, such as local or national government departments, charities, or commercial firms, for things that would previously be done by a nearby relative. The family spirit can be destroyed, and relatives (written to at Christmas and birthdays) no longer seem to belong.

The nuclear family parents have complete control over their children to bring them up as they like without interference from the rest of the family. They are not so easily drawn into family quarrels — on the occasions they do meet they are generally pleased to see one another. Nuclear families can form their own social circle and friends, and not feel a duty to go to relatives.

Few families are completely extended or completely nuclear. Most have some relatives fairly near, and some at a distance. For many years now families have been smaller than they were in the past so that most people have fewer close relatives. In any case, telephones and fast easy communications by car, train and air make it simple to keep in touch with relatives if that is what people want.

THE ELDERLY

Since 1900 there have been great strides in health and medical care. Two of the most dramatic and important changes are shown in the charts below. In 1900, of every 65 babies born alive, 8 would be dead before they were a year old: today only one would die. The expectation of life in 1900 was about 56 for women, and 53 for men: today it is 77 and 71.5 respectively.

Obviously more babies are living to grow into adults, and adults are living much longer — the bar charts on the right show the proportion of people in certain age groups in 1901, 1931 and 1981. You can see how the proportion of the most active age group (16-44) is steadily decreasing, while that of those not normally working (65+) is steadily increasing.

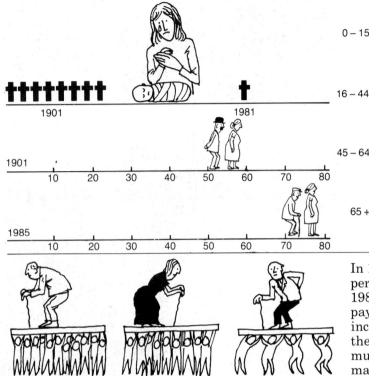

In 1901 there were about 13 workers (16-65) for every person over 65: in 1931 there were 9 workers, and in 1981 only just over 4. As the working population has to pay through taxes to support the people over 65, an increasing burden must fall on them. The problem in the Third World will be even more serious because much of it (unlike the more developed nations) has maintained its traditionally high birth rate.

Problems of the elderly

Physical
Increasing difficulty with movement makes walking, shopping, housework and personal care (washing, dressing) difficult. There is increasing general illness, failing sight and hearing, and a greater risk of accidents.

Financial
A reduced income after retirement may mean a lower standard of living. Older people often have difficulty in understanding changes (e.g. inflation), and worry about paying for food, heating, rent and other essentials.

Emotional
There are emotional problems, especially when a spouse dies. Loneliness and depression are common and forgetfulness can make life very difficult. There may also be severe mental illness through old age.

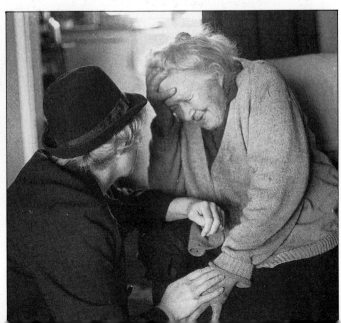

Help for the elderly

In the UK help for the elderly (apart from that by the family) is provided by (1) the State, both national and local government (2) by voluntary organisations such as Age Concern, Help the Aged, religious organisations and schools, (3) private enterprise — firms which specialise in equipment and accommodation for old people (4) self help. In many other societies the elderly depend solely on their families, and great respect is shown to parents and grandparents.

Physical
Homehelps to run the home (State).
Meals on wheels — often run for local authorities by charitable organisations such as WRVS (State).
Regular visits by health visitors for minor health problems and to help in bathing and personal care (State).
Provision of free equipment (walking frames, bathing equipment, hearing aids etc.) to make life easier and to maintain independence (State and Red Cross).

New commercial equipment of all kinds, especially alarm calls which automatically telephone for help in the event of accident or emergency (commercial).
Sheltered accommodation, residential homes, nursing homes when independent life is no longer possible (State, voluntary organisations and commercial).

Financial
Retirement pension increased annually with inflation (State).
Rent and rate rebates (State).
Supplementary pensions if the regular amount is not enough (State).
Heating allowance if necessary (State).
Free medical prescriptions (State).
Free dental treatment and spectacles if the person is drawing supplementary benefit. (State).

Emotional
Day centres and lunch clubs to relieve loneliness (State and voluntary organisations).
Visits by voluntary helpers — Age Concern, Help the Aged, religious organisations, students at school and colleges (voluntary).
Clubs, 'Over-60s' groups, trips (self help).
Reduced-rate holidays in off-peak seasons (commercial).

EDUCATION

Education in its real sense is not an ordeal we have to go through in schools between the ages of 5 and 16 or 18, but something which begins at birth and does not stop until death. It is divided into two main streams — formal and informal, both of which should aim to produce a happy and peaceful society.

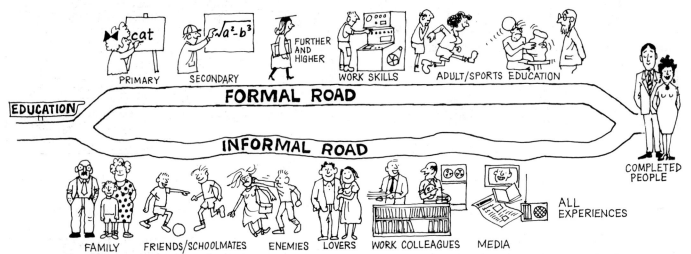

Formal education is the specific facts, skills and attitudes we are taught by teachers and instructors in schools, colleges, work training establishments and adult education centres.

Informal education includes everything we learn almost every moment of our lives from family, friends, enemies, colleagues, entertainments, the media and every experience we have in the world in which we live.

State Education

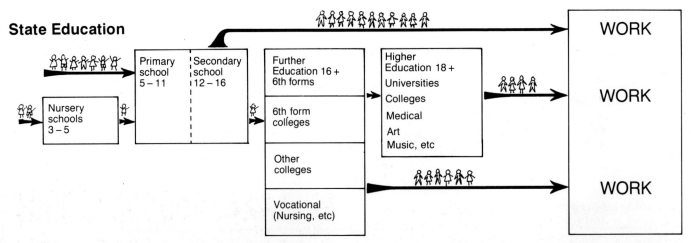

Compulsory formal education begins at 5 years of age and lasts until 16, but there are nursery schools, which are optional from 3 - 5. Compulsory schooling is divided into primary (infants and junior, ages 5 - 11) and secondary (ages 12 - 16). In some areas there are first schools (5 - 8), middle schools (9 - 12/13) and upper schools (13 - 16/18). The age of transfer from one school to another varies slightly in different parts of the country. At the end of compulsory education about 67% of students leave to start work.

Further education — after the age of 16 — consists of the 6th forms in comprehensive schools, 6th form and other colleges, vocational training (e.g. nursing) and other institutions including part-time adult education centres and evening institutes.

Higher education. About 13% of students from further education go on to higher education — universities, colleges of technology, polytechnics, medical schools, teacher-training colleges, some colleges of art and music etc.

Independent schools

About 90% of all students have free education in state schools, but about 10% go to independent schools, either boarding or as day pupils, where at secondary level day fees are about £4500 a year. There are, however, a number of scholarships so that very clever pupils of poorer parents can sometimes go to independent schools free. Parents considering whether to send children to independent or state schools must weigh up the advantages and disadvantages carefully.

Disadvantages
1. Very high cost — at least £100 every school week.
2. Students can lose contact with their family and pick up habits and attitudes their parents do not like or cannot afford.
3. Students mix mainly with others from a narrow social class and are often unable to understand the needs and ideas of people from different backgrounds.
4. Students can become arrogant and feel they have a natural right to be top.

Advantages
1. Usually much smaller classes and more individual attention.
2. More out-of-school activities to broaden students' experience.
3. Highly-selective — often with a high proportion of bright students, and high academic standards.
4. Contacts made at school are often useful later in life — the Old School network.

Equality and inequality in education

In general better education leads to better-paid and more pleasant jobs, a better life-style with a greater range of leisure activities. In the education race everyone is said to start with equal opportunities, and certainly it is possible for a boy or girl from any family background to get the highest education in the country. But in practice something seems to go wrong.

About 7 people in every 20 come from the middle classes (socio-economic groups A, B and C), but at university 15 out of every 20 students come from these groups. About 16 out of 20 MPs of all parties have middle-class backgrounds: among higher management the proportion is still larger.

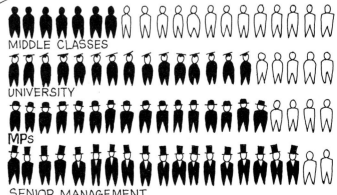

Handicapping in the educational stakes

There are many reasons, most of them outside schools, why educational opportunities are not always equal.

Some students have to do homework and study in a ▶ general living room against TV and general family noise. Others may have a quiet private room.

Interested parents may take children on educational visits, foreign holidays and provide plenty of reference books. Other students may get nothing.

◀ Some students who are having difficulty can get help from their parents: others have parents who are unable to help or who do not care.

Pupils whose parents can afford independent schools often have smaller classes and much more individual attention.

Some children have better physical and emotional care ▶ than others.

Some students have less stable backgrounds than others — broken homes, one-parent families, or very bad conditions.

◀ Some ethnic groups suffer at school for many different reasons.

Some students have physical, mental or psychological handicaps.

Schemes to improve equality in education

Children from deprived homes receive help from local authorities — early entry to nursery schools, family helpers, advice, free milk and free school meals etc.

Special schools exist with specially trained staff (or special facilities in ordinary schools) for students with mental, physical or emotional handicaps. Child guidance clinics are provided to identify pupils with special problems.

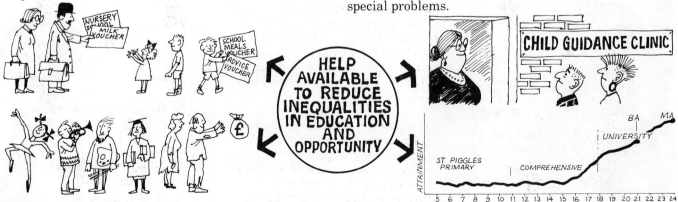

Financial help for the family of students over 11 to enable children to go to the most suitable school or college — academic, music, ballet, art or university.

Comprehensive schools and abolition in most places of the 11+ examination so that 'late developers' are not deprived of the chance of an academic education.

HEREDITY AND ENVIRONMENT

People, both mentally and physically, are shaped by two main forces: heredity and environment.

Environment is the shaping of our personalities and characters by upbringing and surroundings. A person who is brought up in a violent home may well be violent as an adult: a person whose early life is quiet and gentle will probably be the same as an adult. Over-strict or over-indulgent families can have a marked effect on the people we become. Relatives, the neighbourhood, school; all have an effect on the individual.

Heredity is that part of our make-up we inherit from our parents and grandparents. Everyone can see that we have red/brown/black hair like our mother, and grey/blue/green eyes like our father. Some of our features and physique may resemble that of one parent or the other: some may be a mixture of both.
But when it comes to such things that are difficult, or impossible, to see or measure — intelligence, aggression, determination etc. — some people say that these depend much more on the way we were brought up (environment) than on heredity.

Scientists and sociologists argue endlessly on which has the most effect on a person — heredity or environment. There are three main arguments:

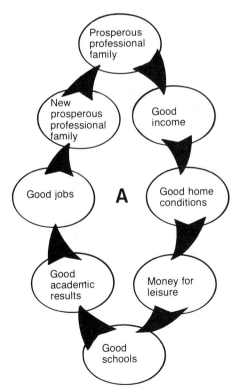

1. The most important influences on a person's character are the qualities received by heredity from parents and grandparents. These may be influenced to a small extent by the environment but 'blood will out.'

2. In intelligence/personality we are all similar at birth but environment is responsible for making us what we grow up to be. A child adopted at birth from brutal parents by a loving couple will grow up as gentle and peaceful as their own natural child.

3. Our genetic make-up predisposes us to behave in a certain way, but this has to be brought out by upbringing, just as a seed will grow into a certain plant, but only if given the right conditions of heat, light, moisture and soil.

How can chain B be broken?

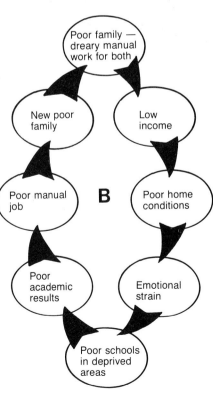

19

Housing

The majority of families in Britain live in homes which consist of a kitchen, a living room, 2 - 4 bedrooms, bathroom and toilet, but the buildings in which these rooms are situated vary widely. There can be detached, semi-detached or terraced houses or bungalows, or flats.

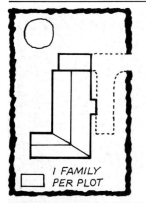

I FAMILY PER PLOT

Detached houses. These are single houses built on a plot of land and not joined to any other.

Advantages
1. Privacy and quiet.
2. Flexible — house and garden can be designed as the owner likes.

Disadvantages
1. Expensive to build — owner has to pay for the whole plot and services.
2. Expensive to maintain, decorate and heat.

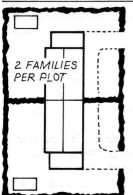

2 FAMILIES PER PLOT

Semi-detached houses. These are pairs of houses joined by a common wall.

Advantages
1. Cheaper because the plot, part of the building, services and maintenance are shared by two families. Heat losses may be lower.

Disadvantages
1. Less privacy. Possibly noise from, and disputes with, neighbours.
2. Less flexible for planning gardens, garages etc.

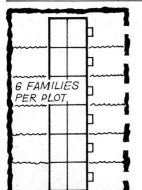

6 FAMILIES PER PLOT

Terraced houses. These are three or more houses joined side-by-side.

Advantages
1. Cheaper to build and maintain because a plot and services are shared by a number of homes.
2. Heat losses can be lower.

Disadvantages
1. Less privacy and more noise — neighbours on both sides.
2. Gardens must be narrow.
3. Difficulty of building garages close to the house. Bicycles and prams have often to be brought in through the front door.

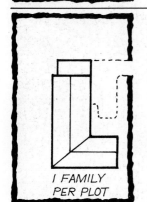

I FAMILY PER PLOT

Bungalows. These are homes built on one level.

Advantages
1. No stairs makes them very suitable for elderly or handicapped people.
2. Cleaning, decoration and maintenance easier because all on one level and no long ladders needed.

Disadvantages
1. More expensive than a house of the same size as a bungalow takes up more land.
2. Some people are nervous of sleeping on the ground floor.

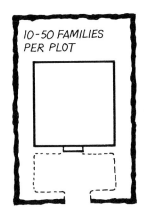

10-50 FAMILIES PER PLOT

Flats. These are a number of homes in a single building. Sometimes this is a large older house which has been converted, but more often it is a specially designed building. Custom-built blocks of flats can be low-rise (up to 6 floors) or high-rise (up to 40 or more floors). Each home is generally on one level, like a bungalow.

Advantages

1. Many more people can be accommodated on a given ground area — very important in cities where land is expensive. This enables more people to live in cities where there is more work.

2. As the ground area and services are shared by many people, the cost to each is often less.

Disadvantages

1. There can be problems of noise from neighbours all round.

2. Lack of privacy: stairs and hallways are often shared.

3. Access problems — lifts not working and difficulty with bicycles and prams.

4. Often there is nowhere for children to play; adults can feel a sense of isolation, especially in high-rise buildings.

High-rise flats.

During World War II hundreds of thousands of houses were damaged or destroyed. Hundreds of thousands of returning servicemen wanted homes of their own. Local authorities too felt that many of the undamaged older houses in cities were no longer fit to live in because they had no bathrooms, inside toilets or running hot water. Many of the city slums were demolished, and there was a frantic re-building programme.

The planners decided that high-rise blocks of flats were the answer: they could be put up quickly and fairly cheaply by new building techniques and could house large numbers of people in a small area. The new flats were certainly of a much higher standard than the small slum houses they replaced: for the first time many people had good sanitation, bathrooms, hot and cold water and central heating. But often the planners

had neglected the personal element: many people found themselves among complete strangers where no community spirit existed. There was no 'popping in next-door for a chat': older people and mothers with small children found themselves almost prisoners because of the difficulty of lifts and stairs. In addition to the emotional problems many people were physically afraid of living high above the ground, and were terrified of fires. As a result there was a great deal of mental and emotional stress: tension and frustration caused widespread violence and vandalism. Many authorities now believe that the high-rise programme was a mistake, and a number of taller blocks are now being demolished in favour of low-rise blocks or estates of semi-detached houses.

NEW TOWNS AND URBAN DECAY

Since the end of World War II the Government has decided that some industries and people should be encouraged to leave the old, congested and over-crowded cities, especially inner-city slum areas and to move to places where there is more space and better conditions and communications. To do this the New Towns Act, 1946, authorised the creation of 23 new towns, usually based on villages or small country towns. Other schemes to disperse industry and people from the decaying urban areas are expanding towns, overspill towns and enterprise zones. Now that many of the worst parts of the older cities have been cleared some authorities are preferring to redevelop these areas with new housing, office blocks and light industry, and to slow down the expansion of other towns.

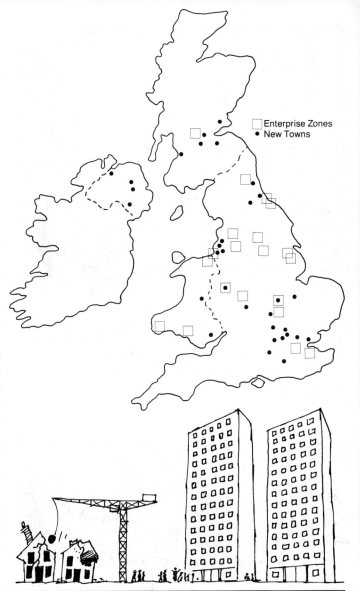

☐ Enterprise Zones
• New Towns

New towns are planned and built by Development Corporations, who sell or rent the houses, factories and shops to people and businesses moving in to the area. The populations range from about 50 000 to 200 000. The towns are naturally very modern, with large pedestrian shopping precincts, new houses and planned estates and parks. The factories are usually light industry — electronics, plastics, and small engineering works. New towns tend to attract younger people, so that there is a high birthrate and low death rate.

Enterprise zones. In some areas the older industries — steel, iron, coal, docks and shipbuilding — are being run down because they are not needed so much or because better production methods are being used. These areas are decaying, with high unemployment, poor housing and derelict premises. The Government encourages new and different industries to move in, offering tax reliefs, and fewer planning controls. Liverpool, Belfast, Clydebank, London docks, Hartlepool and Corby are among the enterprise zones.

Expanding towns. These are medium sized towns whose councils have agreed to take large numbers of people from the crowded parts of large cities. The arrangements are entirely between the two councils. The city authorities and not the town pay for the building of the new housing estates.

Overspill towns. Some small towns have been designated by the government as 'overspill towns'. New factories and houses are built and people and businesses from congested city areas are encouraged to go there. In practice they are very similar to expanding towns.

Slum clearance and inner city decay

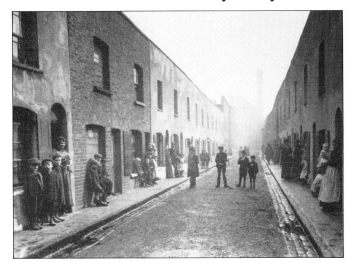

In the nineteenth century many towns and cities grew up round industrial sites — factories, docks and railway centres. Because there was no transport except walking, the homes of the workers were built in tightly-packed terraces as close to the workplace as possible. They were bad even when built — tiny, cramped and without piped water and sanitation — and over the years they grew worse: they were the slums.

In the early twentieth century there were some improvements: the roads were tarred, mains water, electricity and gas were generally installed, and most had flush lavatories, even if these were outside in the back yard. But they were still far below the standard expected of housing in the mid-twentieth century. In addition, many of the industries on which the people had depended had gone — either their goods and services were no longer needed, or else they had moved to more efficient sites. So, in the 1950s many local authorities began major schemes of rehousing the people in newly-built estates of semi-detached houses round the edges of the cities or new towns, or else in huge blocks of flats. The old slum areas were demolished and many redeveloped as new industrial sites, office blocks or better housing.

Very many people did appreciate the new surroundings, but many others missed the warm social and community life of the older crowded neighbourhoods. Relatives and close friends, who had lived nearby in the slums, were often split up on different estates or flats. Many people were complete strangers, and unfriendly because they all felt insecure and isolated. Often work, shops, entertainments, and other facilities were some distance away. Younger people especially often found very little to do.

The rehoused families certainly had better living conditions. They had more space: their homes now had modern sanitation, plumbing and kitchens, and often central heating. Houses on the estates had gardens, and the estates themselves were often planned with open spaces, lawns and trees. But perhaps the middle class planners and architects had designed the new housing more for what they themselves wanted, rather than the people who were being moved.

Questions

The family and the individual

1. Socialisation

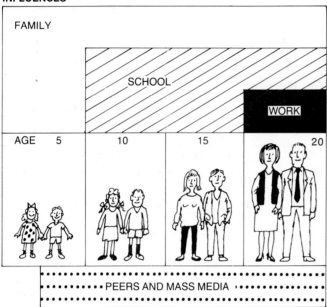

FORMAL INFLUENCES

FAMILY

SCHOOL

WORK

AGE 5 10 15 20

• • • PEERS AND MASS MEDIA • • • •

INFORMAL INFLUENCES

("The Family" — Richard Cootes)

(a) From what age approximately do peer groups influence a person?

(b) Which influence shown above is in operation throughout a person's life?

(c) What is the difference between 'formal influences' and 'informal influences'?

(d) From your Social Studies work, describe what socialisation is and how it affects the whole of a person's life.

'2. Socialisation

"What are little boys made of? Frogs and snails, and puppy-dogs tails, that's what little boys are made of."

(Nursery Rhyme)

(a) What picture of boys is given in the above rhyme?

(b) Give *two* examples of ways parents might treat boy babies differently from girl babies.

(c) Explain how school can reinforce traditional images of male and female roles.

(d) Name and describe *two* laws which have attempted to introduce sexual equality in society.

3. Child development

(a) Why are the first five years of a child's life so important for his/her later development?

(b) Give examples of some of the things which children learn from influences both inside and outside their families during these early years.

(c) How does the upbringing of children in our society differ from that of children in any other society which you have studied?

4. Marriage and divorce

(a) Why do many marriages break up? Upon what grounds may a couple end their marriage in Britain today?

(b) Divorce is on the increase because the idea of marriage is being taken less seriously. Discuss.

(c) Why do some teenage marriages end in divorce?

5. Marriage and divorce

Number married per 1000 by age — England & Wales.

Age Group	Males				Females			
	1941	1953	1964	1975	1941	1953	1964	1975
15-24	70	125	150	151	140	272	302	303
25-34	640	720	765	768	658	798	860	862
35-44	855	862	863	863	752	820	874	877
45-54	847	877	879	879	720	759	809	813
55-64	795	850	860	861	619	624	668	673
65+	619	664	709	711	341	352	341	342

(a) What trend is evident in the rate of marriage and does any age group vary from this general trend?

(b) Is there any evidence of a change in the age of marriage?

(c) What impact do you forsee these changes having on the pattern of family life?

(d) What difference do you see in the age of marriage by the different sexes? How can the difference be explained?

6. The family

Read this extract from 'Just Like a Girl' by Sue Sharpe and answer questions a) and b) which follow it.

"Parents are usually quite unaware of a lot of their own efforts in the manipulation and production of sex differences. They believe themselves to be responding to innate differences that they presume to be present, and interpret similar behaviour differently for each sex. For instance, the way in which parents discipline their children may differ in that boys have more physical punishment and girls more often suffer the withdrawal of parental love and affection. Discipline may also be allocated more often to fathers for boys, and to mothers for girls ...... It is resonable to assume that if girls do tend to be disciplined more like this, then this would increase the need for affectionate relationships and dependency .... Girls generally receive more affection, more protectiveness, more controls and greater restrictions. They are not encouraged to be dependent, but the relative lack of encouragement or opportunity for independence and autonomy has equivalent effects .... Whatever intricate operations are involved in the relationship between parent and child, there is much evidence that boys and girls are taught differently with different roles and goals in mind."

S Sharpe, 'Just Like a Girl'

(a) Carefully explain what the author means in this extract.

(b) Briefly describe how any *two* social institutions other than the family contribute to gender socialisation.

7. The family

(a) Describe, with the help of examples, the traditional roles of men and women within the family in Great Britain.

(b) In what ways have these roles been changing during the course of this century?

(c) What effects have these changes had on the different members of the family?

8. The elderly

Elderly population in thousands

		1911	1931	1951	1971
elderly men aged 65 and over		964	1470	2251	2757
elderly women aged 65 and over		1915	2960	4599	6141
total elderly		2879	4420	6850	8890
elderly as a percentage of the total population		6.8%	9.6%	13.6%	16.0%

(a) In what year were there 2,251,000 men over the age of 65 years old?

(b) How many women over the age of 60 were there in 1931?

(c) In which year did the total elderly account for nearly 10% of the population?

(d) It can be seen from the chart that more people are living to be older. Why do you think this is and what effects may this have on British life in the future?

9. The elderly

"A further increase in the number of 'Senior Citizens' (over 65 years of age) is expected and, if medical advance continues, this could become quite a large increase, since old people would live much longer."

K Heasman 'The Study of Society'

(a) Why is the number of Senior Citizens increasing?

(b) Describe two of the problems which old people face.

(c) How does the state help to solve these problems?

(d) An ageing population, together with a probable earlier age of retirement, will cause problems for society.
Discuss these problems and suggest ways of overcoming them.

10. Education

"Alongside social changes in the 19th century came the pressure for more education by the state for working-class children. The religious pressure for the advancement of state education continued to play a strong role in all schools. Employers realised that the new technical processes which were advancing rapidly demanded a more highly skilled labour force and, as more people were being allowed to vote, the government felt it was important for people to be able to read about and understand political issues".

Beecham/Fiehn/Gates 'Childhood'

(a) According to the passage, support for the development of state education in the 19th century came from three groups in society. Name the three groups.

(b) What reasons did these three groups have for wanting more development of state education?

(c) From your study of education in Britain today, describe the ways in which schools play a part in preparing pupils for their future lives.

11. Education

CSE and GCE Summer Examinations: Entries and Results, England and Wales, Thousands & Percentages

	1962 Boys	1962 Girls	1972 Boys	1972 Girls
Number of entries				
CSE Grade 1			742	608
GCE 'O' Level	1,009	824	1,205	1,100
GCE 'A' Level	184	86	279	188
Results (Percentage of entries)				
CSE Grade 1			15	17
GCE 'O' Level pass	57	58	58	63
GCE 'A' Level pass	66	70	68	71

(Source: Statistics of Education)

Girls are more likely to leave school at sixteen than boys.

(a) How many boys were entered for a) CSE and b) GCE O-L in 1972?

(b) How many girls were entered for a) CSE and b) GCE O-L in 1972?

(c) Give reasons why:
1 Fewer girls than boys take CSE and GCE exams.
2 Girls are more likely to leave school at 16 than boys.

(d) State the changes that have taken place since 1972 (legal, social etc) and say whether you think girls are more equal today 1984.

12. Housing

Types of housing by ethnic groupings

	West Indian %	Asian %	General Population %
Owner-occupied	50	76	50
Council rented	26	4	28
Privately rented	24	19	22
Other	1	1	0

(1981 Census Figures)

(a) Which group of people are more likely to own their own houses?

(b) 26% of which group of people live in council rented housing?

(c) Taking the general population as a whole, which type of housing is the least popular?

(d) Write all you can about why minority groups or the poor tend to live in the worst housing conditions often in the middle of cities.

13. Housing

Describe poor housing conditions in urban areas and say how you would like to see an improvement. Who should be responsible for this improvement?

14. New towns

What are 'New Towns', and why were they built? — How effective are they in solving problems of overcrowding and employment.

Social behaviour

GROUPS

Human beings seem to need to belong to groups. Sociologists divide these into two kinds:

Primary groups. These are normally small enough for a close personal relationship with other members and the whole group feels a strong sense of solidarity. All of the members are very conscious of belonging to that group, and are usually dependent on one another.

Examples of primary groups are the family, clubs, friends, peers, and gangs. A small ethnic or other minority — say a few Asian families in one street, or a dozen Chinese in a large all-white school — may also form a primary group.

◀ **Secondary groups.** These are larger and looser organisations to which people belong often because they have no alternative — schools, firms, trade unions, neighbourhood, racial groups and even social classes. Secondary groups can however be joined voluntarily — support for the local town or county sports team, or the national team in international contests for example. The secondary groups still have the unity and many of the rules and pressures of the smaller primary groups.

Everyone, of course, belongs to many groups simultaneously, both primary and secondary. There is the family, the neighbourhood, the school, the workplace, the clubs, the pubs, friends, gangs, political parties, churches, sports teams and hobby groups. Every individual can behave quite differently as a member of the different groups to which he or she belongs — the gentle father at home can be the ruthless 'killer' at the boxing club, the modest retiring member of the church choir can be the militant trade union official and so on. ▶

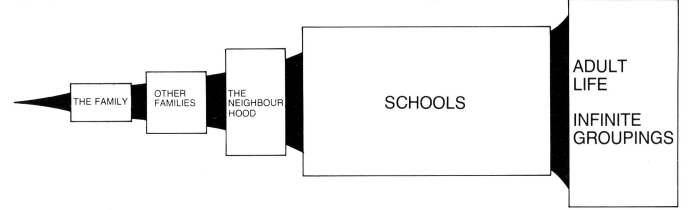

Human babies are born completely selfish and unrestrained. The first group they meet is the family, where they learn that other people have rights too, and that they must conform to rules they do not like: they must not eat with their hands; must not wet on the carpet; must not torment animals; must not smash granny's glasses.

Later they meet other family groups and learn that some of the rules there are different: some children are allowed to do things they are not, and vice versa. Primary and secondary schools provide a widening range of groups and behaviour patterns: there are the swots, the sports fanatics, the smokers, the bullies, the flirts, the teacher-teasers, the teacher-helpers and so on. All of these help to train children for the much more complex groupings of the teenage and adult world.

Why people form groups

The need for security — they feel safer and more confident as one of a group of similar people. Their personality merges in the group's: the decisions — and the blame — are the group's.

They enjoy the companionship of people with the same interests, the same attitudes, the same ideas and the same aims. Joint operations can be much easier than individual ones.

They can often achieve results as part of a group which they could not on their own. This may be partly the group effort, and partly the extra confidence that the group gives them.

In-groups and out-groups

One of the characteristics of a group is that it likes to think its members are 'special' (the in-group) while everyone else is in some way shut out or inferior (the out-group). Groups like to have special signs to show membership, and to distinguish them from the out-groups. These can be uniforms (scouts, guides), badges, clothing and hair styles (punks, skin-heads, pin-stripe suits, rolled umbrellas, Old School ties), behaviour patterns (using certain pubs or restaurants) or special gestures (Nazi-type salutes, communist clenched fist).

27

Often the in-group likes to have secret signs of membership such as special handshakes, passwords, codes, and gestures recognised only by the group. The secrecy emphasises the bond between the members, and excludes non-members more strongly.

This strong bond between members of an in-group makes them feel very differently about the out-group, even when both are doing the same thing or behaving in the same way. It also makes them find excuses or scapegoats when the aims of their group are defeated: 'their' team was unfairly beaten — the referee was against them, or their opponents cheated. They vandalise telephone boxes because they are 'bored' — the out-group (that is the rest of the community) does not provide entertainment for them: smashing up bus shelters is 'youthful high spirits' however much the out-group may call it hooliganism.

Group behaviour

RULES FOR THE CITY GENT GROUP

RULES FOR THE TRENDY LEFTIE GROUP

Groups can survive only if the members conform to the 'rules'. These include behaviour, dress, attitude, and objectives: a person in formal school uniform would not be acceptable to a group of punks, nor a punk in a boy scout troop. A National Front member would not be acceptable to a church youth group in a multiracial area, nor a member of the Militant Tendency in a Young Conservative club.

Pressure on members to conform is very strong, and people often behave in a way that is alien to their normal life-style: those who thoroughly dislike heavy smoking, heavy drinking or drug-taking often do these because they are done in the group to which they belong, or want to belong. They may prefer formal dress, but will wear outlandish garments because the group's expectations demand it: they may struggle to speak in a certain way — either with a pronounced accent, or without any — if that is the group's 'norm'. Members accept these and many other restrictions on their personal liberty and feelings because they want to be accepted, or respected by, or popular with, other people whom they admire. Some fear the consequences if they do not conform — usually these mean expulsion from the circle: it is often much easier, especially in the teens, to follow group thinking and behaviour than to take an individual line.

THE GROUP

Belonging to a group can relieve the individual of much of the responsibility of making decisions, which are made by the group, or its leader. This can be for good, or evil.

Belonging to a group can give an opportunity of leadership, or else of living in a society where decisions are made democratically.

Sharing a common interest can give great satisfaction and enhance the pleasure. The group offers security, and may encourage a more positive attitude; gives confidence — the individual will do things as part of a group he or she would not do alone. This again can be good or bad according to the group.

Individuals learn from the joint activities of the group and may then practise these in personal life.

ETHNIC GROUPS

HIGHEST ETHNIC CONCENTRATIONS

1) Greater Manchester
2) South Yorkshire
3) Birmingham — West Midlands
4) East Midlands — Leicester
5) London
Source: Regional Trends

About 5% of the total population of Great Britain is of New Commonwealth (India, Africa, Caribbean) or Pakistani origin. Overall this is not a large proportion but they tend to be concentrated in certain areas, which can cause problems for both communities.

The map shows the areas with the highest densities of population of New Commonwealth origin. They settle here for reasons of:

Security. As minorities they feel isolated and threatened — often with good cause — and feel safer if they are near people of the same background.

Culture. When there are considerable numbers, there are shops selling ethnic foods, cinemas with films in their own language, mosques and temples for their own religion.

Work. Certain regions attract them because of the main type of work there. For example, Asian peoples are traditionally skilled in textile manufactures, so that it is natural they should settle in Yorkshire.

Some causes of racial conflict

The basic causes of racial conflict are fear, prejudice and ignorance on both sides.

Colour/appearance

Most people of New Commonwealth origin are immediately distinguishable by colour, and sometimes by traditional clothes. People from Russia, for example, whose culture could be completely different from the British, would be not recognised immediately because their pigmentation is European. Colour is the trigger which fires all the old prejudices and misunderstandings.

Language

Asians often talk in their own language among themselves. This at once creates suspicion among those who do not understand — 'They are making fun of us ... they are saying things about us ...' All the racial and other prejudices are immediately reinforced.

Culture

This embraces a vast range of activities, from language and clothing, through leisure activities, working methods and family relationships, even food. Many white people cannot understand the attitudes of some Asians with regard to closely-knit ties and disciplines of the family. They criticise arranged marriages, and the way many ethnic groups mix only with the others of the same race. The natural exuberance of young blacks is sometimes considered as being aggressive and lacking in consideration for others. Some white people think that being different is being wrong.

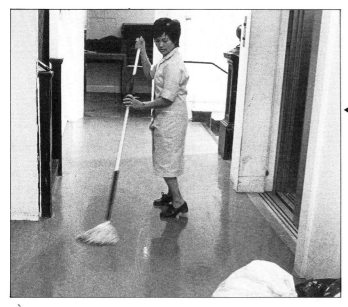

Religion

Although the majority of white British people do not attend church themselves, they often feel strongly about other beliefs. They find excuses, often completely incorrect, for criticising other religions. 'That religion tells them to kill animals cruelly . . . won't let them wear crash helmets like the rest of us . . . treats their women badly . . . worships idols . . .' Their ignorance makes them fear, hate or despise other faiths — and the people who practise them.

◄ Employment

For a variety of reasons (see page 49) much of the work available to ethnic groups is manual. Here they tend to come directly into competition for jobs with a section of white society which is frequently the most highly insecure. The Whites fear they will lose their jobs: the ethnic groups resent the high unemployment among their community — often twice or three times as much as among the Whites.

Housing

Ethnic groups are often bitter at often being more or less confined to poorer housing in decaying inner city districts. The vicious circle of poorer conditions often leads to poorer educational and other facilities, poorer jobs (or unemployment), which means still poorer conditions (page 32). Although it is against the law, white people in 'smarter' areas can sometimes prevent more prosperous ethnic families buying houses in 'their' street.

Race Relations Act 1976
This Act was passed to try to ensure that all races are treated fairly, but it may take many years for prejudice to vanish from our society.

31

FAMILY PROBLEMS

The Nackwurdles — a problem family. All unemployed or unemployable, with individual problems.

| Pa:
alcoholic | Ma:
70-a-day | Nancy:
on drugs | Norman:
violent, hooligan | Nigel:
deprived | Nikker: no known
problems except
wetting the carpet
and biting police. |

All families have some problems — it is quite natural — but the Nackwurdles have most of the serious ones in one family. Society must recognise that (1) social conditions are a major cause of family problems, (2) some families and individuals are less able to cope with their problems than others.

Many perfectly normal well-balanced families have some — or even all — of these problems, for which no-one is to blame. The cause may well be in society itself.

Pressures on the family

Drugs		Teenage rebellion
Poverty		Poor housing
Handicap		Deprivation

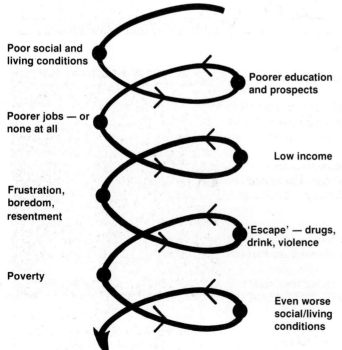

Poor social and living conditions

Poorer education and prospects

Poorer jobs — or none at all

Low income

Frustration, boredom, resentment

'Escape' — drugs, drink, violence

Poverty

Even worse social/living conditions

Social deprivation as a cause of problems

Families with low income, unskilled jobs, or no jobs at all, will often have bad social conditions — poor housing and over-crowding. This generally leads to poorer educational achievement, which in turn means more low-paid jobs or unemployment for the next generation. Unemployment or unsatisfying work means frustration, boredom, and often resentment. To escape from these things the family may turn to excessive drinking, smoking, gambling or drugs. All of these lead to less money for necessities, worse poverty, and even worse social conditions. Resentment and the desire to get money for 'escapes' may lead to crime — with fines, or imprisonment (with loss of job if any) and still more poverty. The whole process spirals downwards.

The poverty trap

Another cause of poverty and bad conditions is the poverty trap, which unfortunately affects those families who are prepared to take low-paid jobs (if they are available) rather than be unemployed. If out of work they will get unemployment benefit, or supplementary benefit. With supplementary benefit they will also have free milk and school meals for the children, free dental treatment, free spectacles, free prescriptions, and rent and rate rebates. If people take low-paid jobs they can fall into the poverty trap: immediately they start to get wages they lose all the benefits, and may well pay tax on their earnings, so that their actual income is lower than when they were unemployed. Family Income supplement is paid by the Government when wages are very low to try to eliminate the poverty trap, but many people ask why they should work for less than they receive if unemployed.

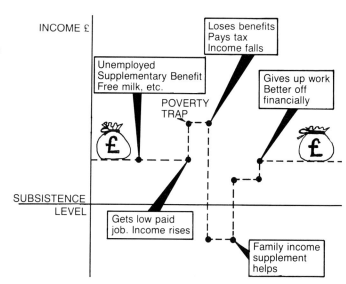

Drugs

Socially-acceptable legal drugs (tobacco, alcohol).
In moderation these can give a great deal of pleasure and make social contacts much easier. But when people drink very heavily, the problems immediately outweigh the benefits.
The family can be driven into debt and lose jobs.
People can become very violent.
Children can lose respect for drunken parents and leave home.
Excessive alcohol can cause insanity and death (estimated 5 000 deaths a year).

Smoking is expensive but not normally as costly to a family as heavy drinking . . . *but*
It is more likely to cause illness, time off work, and death — about 100 000 deaths a year are smoking-related.
It can be anti-social. Passive smoking (non-smokers who are forced to be with heavy smokers) is almost as dangerous to health as active smoking.
Tobacco-related diseases put a heavy burden on the health services.

Unacceptable illegal drugs *soft drugs* (cannabis, glue) and *hard drugs* (heroin, cocaine).
Drug use often begins with teenagers: (1) out of curiosity; (2) through pressure by other addicts and pushers; (3) through pressure by friends; (4) to escape from boredom and bad conditions.

A few soft drugs may not have long-term health dangers but others are harmful and often lead to use of the very dangerous hard drugs. These are lethal because they are highly addictive, need increasing doses to get the same effect, and are all extremely poisonous.

Problems of drug-taking
1. All can be dangerous to health. Hard drugs are almost always fatal.
2. People under the influence of drugs can suffer terrible accidents, and commit unintentional crimes.
3. Personality changes can easily make people completely unemployable.
4. Drug-takers can become social outcasts, rejected by their families and society as a whole because of the practical problems.

Help in drug problems
There are a number of private, charity and NHS clinics as well as in-patient hospitals which try to cure drug addiction. The process is long and painful, and very skilled after-care is essential.

THE BIG KILL

HEALTH WARNING
Smoking kills 200 people a day
in England and Wales.

GIVE UP NOW BEFORE IT KILLS <u>YOU</u>

Mental or physical handicap and long-term illness

These can cause mental and emotional suffering to the whole family. Parents may feel a totally unjustified sense of guilt: brothers and sisters may be embarrassed to take friends home, especially in the case of mental handicap.

Handicap throws a great physical burden on the parents, especially the mother. There are difficulties in finding special education, and in transporting the handicapped person to hospitals, clinics or other treatment. A handicapped member of the family may make holidays very difficult and restrict the whole of family life, which often has to revolve around the handicapped person.

Help in handicap

Until fairly recently the family had to cope with little help, but the situation has now improved. There are many specialist organisations for different handicaps — Mencap, Spastics, Aid for the Crippled Child etc. The State provides special education and home teachers: the NHS and Red Cross provide special equipment. Local authorities will often adapt homes to take wheelchairs and other necessary equipment.

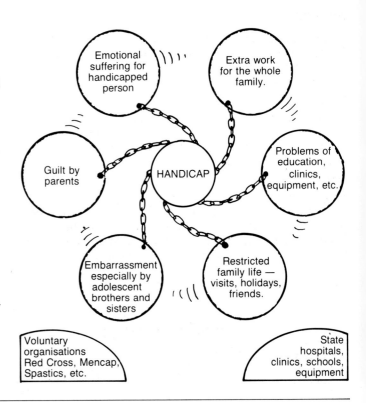

Poor housing and environment

Bad housing means:
1) older buildings without amenities such as bathrooms, hot water and inside lavatories;
2) buildings in a bad state of repair;
3) houses infested with rats or other vermin;
4) some high-rise buildings;
5) houses too close together and general over-crowding.
Some authorities put all of their 'problem' families together on one estate — usually the poorest. This increases the problem — there is no example to follow and no incentive to improve conditions.

Results of bad housing

1. People spend as much time as possible out of the home, in pubs and other places where they may spend more than they can afford, or else they wander the streets, often getting into trouble with police for vandalism.
2. Poor conditions may lead to children being neglected or cruelly treated.
3. Educational standards are often low because there are no facilities or encouragement at home to study.

Help in bad housing

Re-housing by the local authority. This has to be done carefully as many mistakes have been made by planners in the past — high-rise blocks for example. Some new estates have been made into slums in a few years because the authorities had not got to the root of the problem.

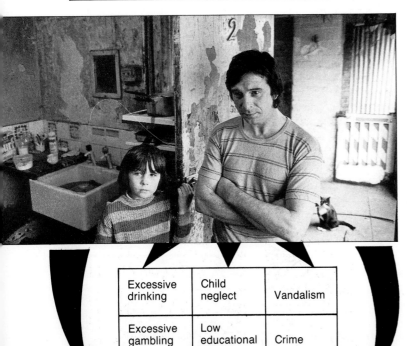

Excessive drinking	Child neglect	Vandalism
Excessive gambling	Low educational standard	Crime

Poverty

In 1987 the poverty line was about £90 a week for a family with two children. But of course, some families can earn much more than this and still live in conditions of poverty.

Poverty conditions are the result of:
1. Low income — unemployment, poorly-paid work.
2. Lack of ability to manage the family budget — extravagant over-spending on non-essential items.
3. Too much of the family income spent on alcohol, tobacco, gambling.

Help in poverty
1. Short-term — payment of supplementary benefits by the state to bring income above the poverty line.
2. Longer-term: the social services department of the local authority may send a social worker from the Family Service Unit to help out physically and also to advise the family on budgeting and management.

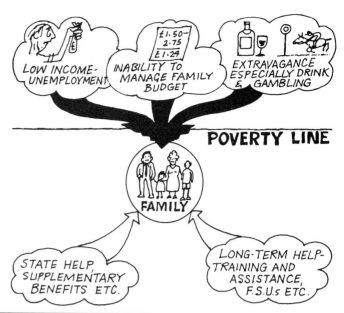

Teenage rebellion

It is natural for adolescents to want independence, but when this is taken together with other problems such as drink, drugs, bad housing and unemployment, it may show itself in:
1. Vandalism
2. Hooliganism, or
3. Crime.

Help in teenage rebellion
The most important help is from the family, but if this is not available child guidance clinics, social workers or probation officers can sometimes help. If these fail the police and courts must intervene with enforced community service and, if necessary, detention centres.

Deprivation

Children can be deprived emotionally or physically, often both together. The parents may have problems with heavy drinking, smoking, drug abuse, poverty, bad housing or mental and emotional difficulties. These problems may result in actual cruelty and neglect to the child, who may have poor clothing and food and insufficient sleep. They can also deprive children of love, attention, emotional contact and discipline, so that they become anti-social, aggressive and out of control.

Help in deprivation
Serious cases of cruelty are of course a matter for the law, and parents can be sent to prison for child abuse. In other cases of neglect — emotional and physical — children may be taken from the parents and sent to local authority homes or placed with foster parents. The best solutions are however to remove the causes of the problem such as housing and poverty, and to try to help the parents to cope with the situation with assistance from voluntary organisations and Family Service Units.

CRIME AND PUNISHMENT

What is crime?

Crime is breaking the laws of the country in which one is living. In general governments pass laws against those actions which they see as injurious to the public welfare — things which are likely to harm, or make unpleasant or unfair the lives of most people, or to make society unstable. If theft were not illegal, no-one's property would be safe; if people were allowed to drive without any training at 70 mph, everyone's life would be in danger. Laws are passed to protect society: those who break them are guilty of offences, and are liable to punishment.

The definition of crime must alter with circumstances and changes in society: no government in 1830 would have passed laws fixing a speed limit of 70 mph because as far as they knew nothing could exceed 12 mph. On the other hand, the same government would not have considered stopping children of 3 or 4 going to work underground in coal mines, because they saw nothing wrong in it. Many modern Islamic states make drinking alcohol illegal but permit the smoking of cannabis: western societies do the reverse.

The licence for people to act as they please is limited not only by the laws of the State (crimes), but also by laws of the Church, (sins). Though relatively few people today attend church its teaching has become so much part of the way of life that many crimes are sins, and sins crimes — murder, theft, cheating, for example. But there are some sins which are not crimes: in the Christian faith adultery, working on Sundays, not respecting parents and being jealous of ones neighbours are sins, but not crimes. In other faiths there are other differences.

Causes of crime

There are thousands of ways of breaking the law, but almost all crimes are caused by one or more of six basic reasons.

Greed. Crimes for profit range from stealing a 5p bar of chocolate to great financial swindles involving millions of pounds.

Convenience. For instance: motorists' parking and speeding offences; parents keeping children away from school unnecessarily — to help at home or for company.

Excitement. People whose lives are boring may commit crimes for excitement, sometimes under the influence of alcohol or drugs.

On principle. People may believe so strongly in some principle they may be prepared to commit what others call crime — refusing to pay taxes, bombing and assassination.

Grudge against society. Crimes such as vandalism and violence may be caused by people with grudges about bad conditions and deprivation or with personality problems.

Psychological defect, or stress. Mentally unbalanced or disturbed people may commit violent crimes: ordinary people may behave abnormally under stress — e.g. child abuse by parents.

Reasons for rise in crime

This chart shows the increase in major areas of crime over the last 15 years. Only sexual crimes (down 9%) show any decrease. Can you suggest why these should be lower when all other crimes show such large increases? Below are some of the reasons frequently offered to explain the rise in crime: discuss these and suggest others which you think may be relevant.

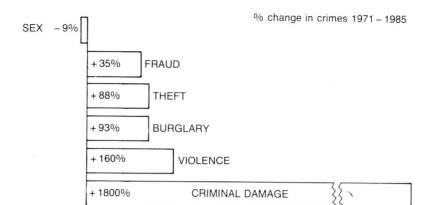

% change in crimes 1971 – 1985

SEX – 9%
+ 35% FRAUD
+ 88% THEFT
+ 93% BURGLARY
+ 160% VIOLENCE
+ 1800% CRIMINAL DAMAGE

Rise in unemployment. People are forced into crime out of necessity because they do not have enough to live on, or at least in the style they grew used to when they were in work.

Decline in family influence (and sometimes religious influence). Parents are concerned only with themselves and do not discipline children, who run wild and into crime.

Inner city decay/deprivation, bad housing and social conditions. These will include some modern housing estates, tower blocks and new towns.

Ethnic problems. Non-white teenagers especially may live in poor conditions and have few job opportunities or prospects. In a hostile society they seem to have few outlets except crime.

Decline in quality of policing. The old style policeman on the beat who knew everyone has been replaced by unknown officers in cars. (Officers who perhaps have ethnic or other prejudices).

Influence of the media. Television crime drama, books, magazines, films and, more recently and importantly, video tapes often glorify violence and are imitated.

Crime, age, and sex

The charts shows the number of persons out of every thousand in the age group who were convicted of crime in 1985 — if one took the number who actually committed crime and were not caught, the figures would be much larger. Notice how the great majority of crimes are committed by people between the ages of 14 -20, with the peak in the 14 - 16 group.

Suggest why you think crime is so high in the teens. What do you think can be done to reduce these figures? Notice how relatively low the numbers are for the over-21s. What causes this sudden and dramatic change to a more law-abiding life in their twenties?

10 – 13	14 – 16	17 – 21	21 +
29/1000 10/1000	81 22	73 12	13 2

Criminal statistics

As we shall see on page 60 all statistics need careful examination before we believe them completely, and none are more suspect than those for crime. By carefully selecting and manipulating the figures the results can be made to look worse, or better, than they really are.

The man below may be horrified that mass murder has increased by 100% in a year, but if he looked at the actual numbers he would see that in one year there was one mass murderer, and the following one two. This *is* an increase of 100%, but it was completely an accident that in two years there should be three people who were totally insane. For the next five years there could easily be no mass murders at all.

Minor offences 1971 – 84

A scare-mongering paper *The Daily Puff* also quotes real government statistics:

'The number of minor offences known to the police rose from 3 418 000 in 1971 to 6 082 000 in 1984...'

The paper comments:

'This staggering increase of 78% means that almost one person in every ten — men, women, children and babies — was guilty of some offence. Britain is fast becoming a nation of criminals, and the few law-abiding citizens are terrified in their beds, let alone in the street...'

The figures given are absolutely correct, but if we look more closely at those for 1984 we find that 75% — three-quarters — were parking tickets. Illegal parking is hardly likely to make law-abiding citizens shiver between the sheets. Another 20% were minor motoring offences, leaving 5% of other minor crimes.

The Daily Puff also attacks the police for inefficiency in clearing up offences. Quoting the government statistics table given below, it says:

'Police inefficiency. In 1971 the police managed to clear up 45% of all serious offences reported. In 1984 it was only 35%. Obviously there is something radically wrong with our policing...'

But if we look at the other government report on the table on the right we find that in 1971 there were 1 665 700 serious crimes notified, while in 1985 there were 3 611 900.

45% of 1 665 700 is 749 565, while 35% of 3 611 900 is 1 264 165, so that in *numbers* the clear-up rate in 1985 had risen by 68%.

You could discuss why the actual numbers of serious crimes had increased so much between 1971 and 1985.

Table 12.1 Notifiable offences recorded by the police by type of offence
England & Wales, Scotland, and Northern Ireland

	England & Wales		
	1971	1984	1985
Notifiable offences recorded			
Violence against the person	47.0	114.2	121.7
Sexual offences	23.6	20.2	21.5
Burglary	451.5	897.5	871.3
Robbery	7.5	24.9	27.5
Theft and handling stolen goods	1,003.7	1,808.0	1,884.1
Fraud and forgery	99.8	126.1	134.8
Criminal damage	27.0	497.8	539.0
Other notifiable offences	5.6	10.4	12.2
Total notifiable offences	1,665.7	3,499.1	3,611.9

Table 12.2 Clear-up rates for notifiable offences: by type of offence
England & Wales, Scotland, and Northern Ireland

	England & Wales		
	1971	1984	1985
Notifiable offences recorded			
Violence against the person	82	74	73
Sexual offences	76	72	72
Burglary	37	28	29
Robbery	42	22	22
Theft and handling stolen goods	43	35	35
Fraud and forgery	83	69	68
Criminal damage	34	23	23
Other notifiable offences	92	93	93
Total notifiable offences	45	35	35

Why punish?

The law punishes people who do wrong for some or all of the following reasons:

Punishment. Society feels that people who do wrong should suffer for the suffering they have caused to others.

Deterrent. Society hopes that by punishing people who are caught in crime it will deter others from doing the same through fear of being caught.

Protection. Society feels that it must protect itself from criminals, especially violent ones, by shutting them away where they can do no harm.

Reformation. Society hopes that punishment will prevent criminals from repeating their crime because they realise it is wrong.

Different sorts of punishment

Reprimand. A 'telling-off' in public may be a severe punishment for people who have held a responsible position or have been respected in the community, especially if the offence is not serious and not likely to be repeated.

Conditional discharge and binding over. Mainly for minor offences when the judge feels that the person has already been punished enough by appearing in court. If the person who has been bound over repeats the offence he or she is taken back to court and sentenced for both offences.

Probation. Convicted persons have to report to the probation officer at certain intervals to show that they have not been in trouble again. This is normally used for people convicted for the first time and who are not regular criminals.

Community service. Mainly for younger offenders. Instead of sending them to prison or borstal they are made to work for the public good, clearing derelict land, repairing or decorating buildings etc.

Fines. Flat-rate fines can be unfair — a fine of £50 might be a large sum to a poor person but scarcely missed by a rich one. Some countries impose fines of a percentage of the person's income.

Taking away privileges. This normally means banning motorists and motorcyclists from driving when they have been convicted of serious traffic offences such as drunkeness or reckless driving.

Suspended sentence. People are given a prison sentence but it may be 'suspended' for up to 2 years. If they get into no more trouble in that time, they do not go to prison at all: if they do get into trouble, they are liable to be sent to prison on both charges.

Prison or custodial sentence. The convicted person is deprived of liberty by being sent to prison, borstal or detention centre. It may be a strict fortress-like prison, or an open prison where the convict is put on trust not to escape.

The welfare state

A Welfare State is one in which the State (both local and national government) organises services to the community to minimise or eliminate as far as possible poverty, disease and the problems of maternity, infancy, education, unemployment, housing, handicap, old age and death. As the Socialist Government of 1945 proclaimed, it provides care 'From the cradle to the grave.'

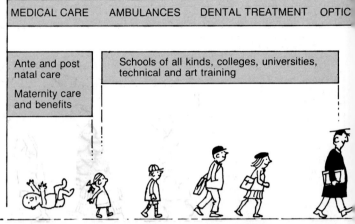

Until the twentieth century the State accepted little responsibility for the social welfare of its citizens. This was left to the family, to charity or, as a last resort, to the parish workhouse or outdoor relief.

In the nineteenth century a slightly more humane spirit was abroad at least in medicine. All doctors had to be paid, but some adjusted their fees so that the rich subsidised the poor. Hospitals, all run by charity, often had schemes whereby poorer people could get some treatment. But no-one had a *right* to any treatment at all. Unemployment, accident, injury, old age and any other disaster were still left entirely to chance or charity.

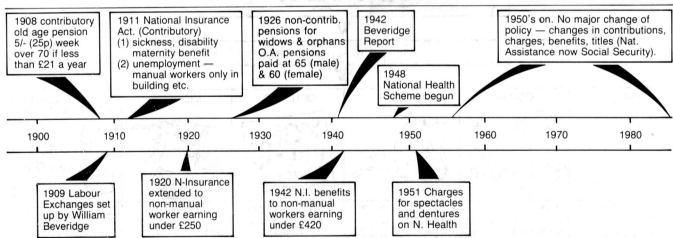

Between 1906-14 the Liberal Government with Lloyd George took steps to organise State social welfare with unemployment, sickness and old age (70+) benefits. Each worker, the employer and the State contributed towards the cost. In 1925 the Conservative Government of Stanley Baldwin extended the scheme: people received an old age pension at 65 (men) and 60 (women), and widows and orphans were also entitled to benefits.

During World War II the National Coalition Government accepted that the State must accept the responsibility of helping to relieve the worst of the

evils. The Liberal, Sir William Beveridge, was asked to draw up a scheme for this and in 1942 the famous Beveridge Report was published. This was put into practice by the Labour government of Clement Atlee when the war ended, and is the basis of much of our present welfare system. Both Beveridge and the Labour government saw the scheme as being self-financing — that is, contributions paid by workers, employers and state would pay for all of the considerably increased benefits. People who were outside the scheme for one reason or another could get assistance from the newly set up National Assistance Board.

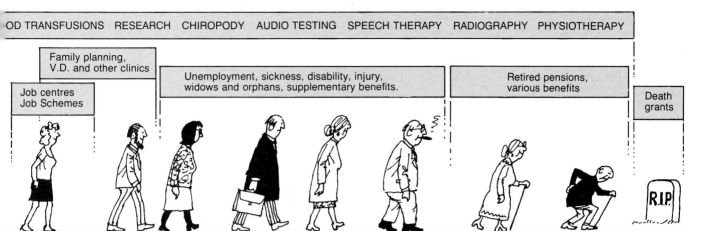

National Health Service (NHS)

A completely free National Health Service began under the Labour Government in 1948, and was immensely successful. Any person, however poor, could now have the most expensive medical treatment. Unfortunately the health service proved more costly than had been expected, and in 1949 the Labour National Insurance Act empowered the government to make charges for medicines, spectacles and other equipment. These charges were introduced by the Conservative Government in 1952. Since then the costs and the scope of the health service have increased rapidly, and governments of both parties have been forced to increase charges. However, because many people — elderly, children, chronic invalids, pregnant women, low-income groups etc — are excluded, only 30% of all patients using the health service actually pay prescription and other charges.

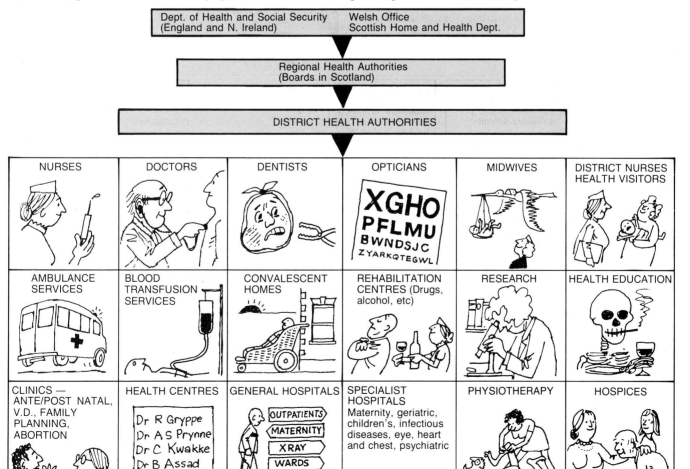

Administration of the NHS

General practitioners/family doctors. The first treatment of patients is by the family doctor, who sometimes works in cooperation with district nurses and social workers. An average NHS doctor with about 2000 patients is paid a flat rate of about £8 per head per year, irrespective of the number of visits the patient makes, or the kind of illness. Extra payments are made for patients over 65 and for work in inner city and rural areas.

Many doctors now have their surgeries in health centres, which are modern purpose-built buildings where there are generally a number of different clinics, rooms for chiropody, audio-testing, speech therapy etc. After examining the patient the doctor may: (1) prescribe medicine and/or treatment; (2) send the patient to a hospital for physiotherapy or X-ray examination; (3) send the patient to a hospital to see a consultant, either as an in-patient or as an out-patient.

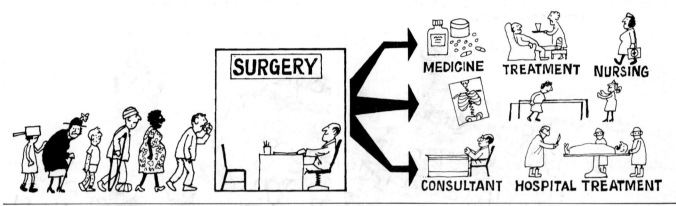

Financing the NHS

The NHS is not cheap: it costs about £17 500 000 000 a year — about £300 for every person in the country. National Insurance contributions vary, but a typical employee pays £18 each week, and the employer £21. Although this may seem high, it is less than half the amount an average person pays in the United States, where there is no similar government health scheme covering everyone.

The NHS, Social Security and Personal Social Services, make up the bulk of what we call the Welfare State. The total cost of this in 1985/6 was about £57 billion, of which the NHS took £16 bn. National Insurance contributions produce about only £18 bn, so that the remaining £39 bn comes from general taxation and from charges for prescriptions, dental treatment and spectacles. In practice, about 90% of the NHS is funded by general taxation.

Approximate costs to NHS of patients in different age groups, per year.

AGE	Under 1	1 – 4	5 – 15	16 – 24	25 – 44	45 – 65	65 – 74	75 +
Cost	£526	£204	£130	£138	£157	£230	£473	£1087

Personal social services provided by local authorities

For children. Local authorities should provide:
1. Day nurseries and nursery schools or classes for children under school age.
2. Residential homes (or foster homes) where children can live until they are 18 if for some reason their own homes are unsuitable.
3. Family aid and social workers to help families which are having problems — single parent families, families which are generally incapable of coping with difficulties of money or everyday life.

For the mentally handicapped and mentally ill.
Authorities should:
1. Set up residental and social centres for patients both before and after hospital treatment.
2. Provide training centres where the handicapped can learn social habits and such manual skills that they are capable of — simple crafts.
3. Provide social workers to give help and advice to families of the mentally handicapped.

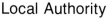

Local Authority
County Council

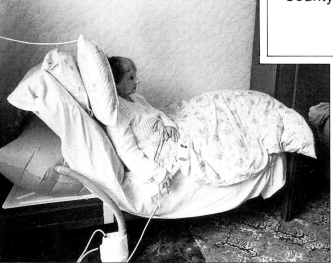

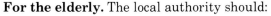

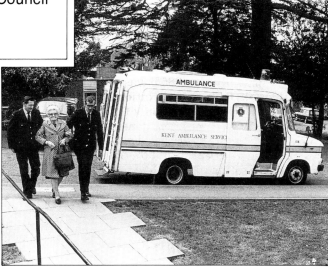

For the elderly. The local authority should:
1. Find out from social workers the extent of the problem in the area.
2. Provide purpose-built accommodation, some with wardens, for people no longer capable of living on their own.
3. Provide home-helps, laundry services, meals-on-wheels, night attendants and other services for elderly people who with these aids are still capable of living in their own homes.
4. Set up day centres and social clubs, with cheap transport to them, to enable the elderly to continue social life and not to remain house-bound.

For the physically handicapped. Local authorities should find out how many such people there are and make sure they know the services available. These include:
1. Providing social workers to advise on personal and social problems connected with the handicap.
2. Adapting homes — widening doorways, providing ramps for wheelchairs etc.
3. Providing special equipment to allow the handicapped person to live as normal a life as possible — specially adapted baths, toilets, taps, cookers.
4. Providing home-helps to do housework and shopping if necessary.

Welfare — state or private?

Most people will never earn enough to guard themselves against the misfortunes that can happen. They may have accidents, become unemployed or ill — and medical treatment is very expensive. A patient in hospital costs about £90 a day on average, and a simple operation for appendix removal, about £300. People may die early, leaving dependent spouses and children. Few people can save enough in a whole working life to live on in retirement. Many live for 15 or 20 years after finishing work, and in these years medical costs rise sharply.

It seems only fair that the State should provide for all of these basic human needs so that everyone, and not only the wealthy in the country has the same treatment.

The Welfare State is very expensive, taking up almost half of the government's public expenditure. The bureaucracy is also cumbersome and complicated, so that people really in need often do not get the benefits they are entitled to while some scroungers manage to live comfortably on the state without working. Some people grow to be dependent on the State for everything when they are quite capable of helping themselves. National insurance contributions are up to 9% of each employee's income, plus up to another 11% from the employer: if this amount were paid into private medical and pension funds (which might be more efficient than the huge state machine) it might offer better value and benefits.

The welfare scales

Perhaps the answer is to have a mixture of state and private welfare enterprises. Many people today pay extra to have benefits from private medical and pension schemes, as well as from the welfare state. Does this create a two-tier welfare system — a basic one for the poor and a more luxurious one for the rich? Or should people be allowed to spend their money as they like?

Voluntary organisations

Voluntary charity work has always been very important in Britain, and it is estimated that one person in every four is in some way involved in one or other of the organisations. The churches take a leading role, and have many local and national schemes in all aspects of welfare. Below are just a few of the national organisations which are not connected specifically to any religious body.

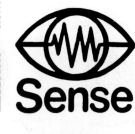

Social security

The idea of social security is to provide a basic income for people who for one reason or another are not able to earn one for themselves. Some social security benefits are contributory — that is, they are given only to people who have paid a certain number of contributions from their wages to the National Insurance scheme when they were working. Other benefits are non-contributory — that is people are given them whether they have contributed or not. Some of these non-contributory benefits are available only after a 'means test' — the authorities check up just how much money the applicants have in income and savings and what their justifiable outgoings are before allowing any payments.

Contributory benefits are: (1) Unemployment benefits for people out of work and their dependents; (2) Benefits for people who are unable to work because of sickness or injury; (3) Maternity benefits for a maximum of 18 weeks; (4) Retirement pensions for women over 60 and men over 65 if they are no longer working. If people are still working they are not eligible for a full retirement pension until 65 (women) and 70 (men); (5) Widows' pension; (6) Death grant.

Non-contributory benefits are: (1) Family allowances and child benefits; (2) Invalid care and mobility allowances for handicapped people; (3) a small single maternity grant. If people still cannot manage, or cannot claim any of these above allowances they may after a means test obtain supplementary benefit and housing allowance. In theory this should eliminate all of the worst poverty, but often desperate need still exists, generally because people are not aware of their rights.

Questions

Social behaviour

1. Family problems

(a) What is meant by the term the "generation gap"?

(b) Give two statements from the text against the parents' interference and two statements in support of parents' interference.

(c) Give three other areas, not mentioned in the text, where parents and their children frequently disagree.

(d) From your social studies work, say whether you think the generation gap actually exists or whether it is a myth.

2. Groups

Teenagers today have more money than ever before to spend on the latest fashions and crazes, and in providing clothes, music and leisure activities for them, businessmen and commercial interests have been able to make a lot of money.

Television, radio, newspapers and magazines have also played their part. By giving lots of publicity to both the good and bad aspects of gang behaviour they've encouraged them to spread. But being part of a gang obviously appeals to teenagers too. Having a group to identify with and spend time with is important, especially if school and the older generation of parents seem out of touch and not interested in the things you enjoy.

*'Studying Society' J.L. Thompson
pub: Hutchinson.*

(a) Which teenage youth movements are most common today?

(b) Describe the clothes, attitudes and activities of one such group.

(c) How does i) Mass Media
                ii) Commercial interests
    react to them.

(d) From your Social Studies work, say what you think the older generation thinks about them.

3. Groups

(a) What is meant by the term "peer group"?

(b) Give *three* examples of other groups to which people belong.

(c) Why is it important for an individual to belong to such groups?

(d) Choosing *one* group with which you are familiar, describe the ways in which its members influence and control one another.

4. Crime

Crime statistics for 1973

Non-indictable offences Persons found guilty		Indictable offences Persons found guilty	
Motoring	1,191,808	Theft & receiving	180,875
Intoxicating liquor	105,200	Burglary	54,362
Taxation	92,997	Criminal damage	32,223
Wireless telegraphy	42,734	Violence	33,041
Highway Act	22,551	Fraud and forgery	16,105
Social security	12,881	Sex offences	7,169
Assault	12,054	Robbery	3,159
Drugs	11,988	Others	9,512
Railways	11,417		
Disorderly behaviour	8,851		336,446
Others	78,741		
	1,591,222		

(a) How many people were found guilty of all crimes which involved the removal of someone else's property?

(b) 92,997 people were found guilty of what crime?

(c) What is the difference between the numbers of people found guilty for indictable and non-indictable offences?

(d) What does the term "non-indictable offence" mean?

(e) From your Social Studies work, what factors sometimes persuade people to take up crime?

5. The Welfare State

"It has been said that the Welfare State helps a person 'from the cradle to the grave'. However, Lord Beveridge pointed out that '. . . . . at certain times of life, families are particularly vulnerable. They tend to pass through similar patterns of need as the years go by'."

K Heasman 'The Study of Society'

(a) Give two examples of vulnerable or difficult periods in family life.

(b) Give two examples of State aid which are available to assist families.

(c) Describe how welfare services are financed locally and nationally.

(d) There are gaps in the Welfare State provision of services. Discuss how these may affect people, and how the gaps may be filled.

Changing social patterns

INCOME AND WEALTH

We all have to have an income whether it comes from wages, salaries, profits, pensions or social security. This chart shows where the family money came from in 1975 and 1984. How do you account for the drop in income from wages and salaries, and the increase from social security?

The weekly earnings before tax vary considerably. Below are the figures for male and female manual and non-manual workers in 1985. How do you account for the differences?

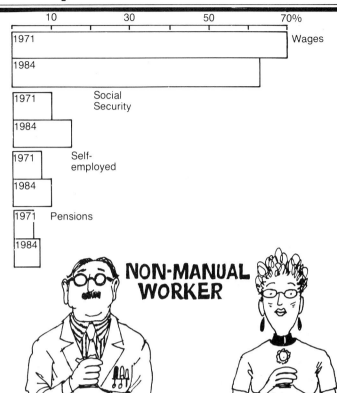

MANUAL WORKER £183 WEEK £124 WEEK

NON-MANUAL WORKER £230 WEEK £140 WEEK

Distribution of wealth

Everyone knows that the wealth of the country is not shared equally among all the people. The chart below shows how the wealth of the country is distributed. Do you think this is right? Should say a pop star have so much more money than a doctor, and a doctor so much more than a road sweeper? What do you think would happen if all the wealth in the country was shared equally among all the people?

78% OF ALL WEALTH — RICHEST 25%
18% OF ALL WEALTH — NEXT 25%
4% — POOREST 50%

Redistribution of wealth

Governments of all parties try to redistribute wealth so that there is not such a gap between the richest and the poorest people. This is done by heavier taxation on the richest, and more benefits for the poorer. The gross income of the richest fifth of the population is over six times as much as that of the poorest. After taxation and benefits have been taken into account, the richest have just over three times as much as the poorest.

GROSS INCOME £3140
TAXES £860
BENEFITS £1340
FINAL INCOME £3620

GROSS INCOME £19240
TAXES £7890
BENEFITS £1580
FINAL INCOME £12,130

SOCIAL INEQUALITY

Society is made up of millions of people, all of whom are completely different. Their individuality is shaped by heredity and environment — and by chance, which can be anything from a change of government to a crippling illness or an accident. Yet all of us fall into a relatively small number of groups — sex, age, race, social class, religion and so on. These groups are often divisive, create inequality and fix our place in society. Membership of some groups will often mean almost automatic membership of others. Upper social class background usually means a higher income, a better job, better housing and better educational opportunities. Membership of some ethnic groups often means less chance of employment, poorer jobs, lower income, poorer housing and so on.

Below you can see a few of the major groupings in society. Some of these, of course, like sex, age and race cannot be altered, while others can. It is the duty of society and governments to try to ensure that membership of any group is not a barrier, and that all people enjoy social justice.

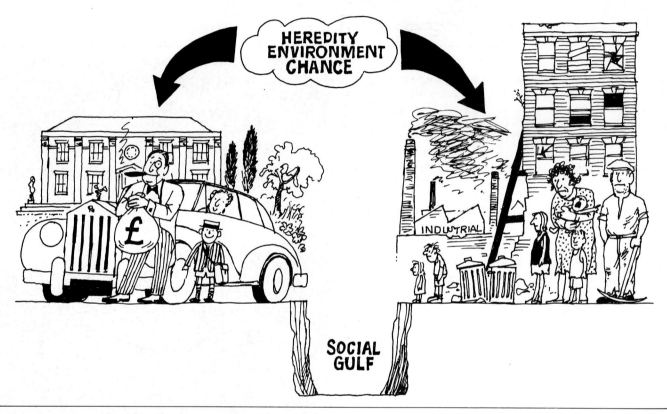

Sex

150 years ago women in Britain had very few legal rights at all. Today laws have given them equality in all respects with men. But in practice there are still differences: there are relatively few women in 'top' jobs; promotion prospects are poorer for women; the average wage of women, despite the Equal Wages Act, is lower than that for men. There are relatively few women in the professions except nursing and teaching. In the home they are often expected to do all of the domestic duties as well as having a paid job.

On the other hand women are often accused of wanting the best of both worlds — legal and professional equality with males, *and* all the privileges they enjoyed when they were considered unequal.

Age

Younger people often resent the authority, wealth and power that usually rests with older people. Young people often say that the older generation do not understand their points of view and impose out-of-date codes on them. At home they may dislike parental discipline: at work they may feel that older people have the better positions and stand in the way of promotion.

Older people can resent the privileges and freedom that younger people have today, and which they did not have at the same age. They may be highly critical of behaviour, dress, morals and general life style of the younger generation.

Race

Just as many women feel that all men gang up against them so many racial groups feel that all white people gang up to exclude Blacks and other ethnic people from equality. As with the differences between men and women, much of the problem comes from traditional prejudices, and fear. Ethnic groups, however, are often faced with an environmental barrier which is very difficult to cross. Low income means poorer housing in poorer inner-city areas, with poorer educational opportunities. This means higher unemployment, which means lower income . . . and the circle goes round again.

The key to the problem is education for all groups to reduce prejudices and to raise standards.

Religion

Practising Christians are a minority in Britain today, and though religion is not as divisive (except for Ulster) today as it was in the past, it is still a factor in some places. In a few areas such as Liverpool and Glasgow the Catholic/Protestant conflict can sometimes lead to bitterness and violence, but today ill feeling is more likely to exist between Christian and non-Christian beliefs. In some places it is easy to whip up anti-Jewish, anti-Moslem or anti-Sikh feelings on the basis of some misunderstood aspect of their religious beliefs or practices. Once again, this is likely to be because of traditional prejudices or fear.

Social class

The British often describe themselves as upper class, middle class and working class. The government refers to them as socio-economic groups A, B, C, D and E. Class is very difficult to define: it often has much to do with wealth and occupation, but not always. A manual worker who won a million pounds would not think he had become upper class, nor would a lord's son earning only £50 a week sweeping roads be considered working class. Class labels can be very emotive and divisive: a judge, a navvy, a bishop and a prostitute all work for a living — are they all working class? In general, people in a 'class' tend to have the same kind of background, the same kind of education, the same kind of spending, leisure and lifestyle. How would *you* define 'class'?

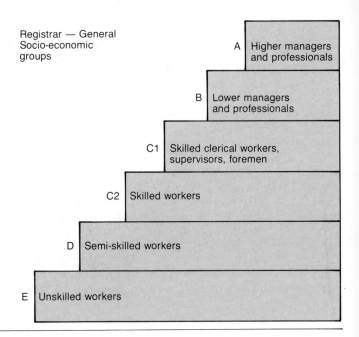

Registrar — General Socio-economic groups

A	Higher managers and professionals
B	Lower managers and professionals
C1	Skilled clerical workers, supervisors, foremen
C2	Skilled workers
D	Semi-skilled workers
E	Unskilled workers

Region

The graph on page 57 shows just one of the many differences between the regions of Britain. Some regions seem to have the worst of almost everything — high unemployment, poorer housing, poorer health, lower wages, shorter life and fewer luxuries than others. In general, the south-east is the most prosperous; the north, Scotland and Ireland the least. This can create inequalities and jealousy. What do you think has caused these differences and what do you think can be done to minimise them?

Wealth

The amount of money a person possesses is bound to create inequality. Family A have an income of £10 000 a week: Family B live on £70 a week social security. Is this just? Does it make any difference if family B refuse to work though quite capable of doing so, and family A work on average 10 hours a day, seven days a week? Does the way in which people acquire their wealth make any difference? Is it right for people to be rich because they have inherited the money? If they have worked for it — say by entertaining millions with music or writing — are they justified in being richer than others? It is said that if all the money in the country were shared out equally, at the end of the next week there would be rich and poor again: do you think there is some truth in this?

Education

There are 'good' schools and 'bad' ones in both the state and private systems. In the state system it is usually a matter of luck whether people live in the 'right' area to go to one of the 'better' schools. In the private system it is a matter of choice — or money. Why should a private school seem to offer advantages? Is it that pupils learn to speak with the 'proper' accent? Or because they have influential friends? Or because the teaching (because of fewer pupils per teacher) can often be better? Or because the boarding system gives some special quality? Should people be allowed to buy private education which seems to offer some advantages in later life? Family A has a larger than average income, but spends most of it on gambling, drinking, smoking, luxury cars and holidays. Family B has the same income but lives very modestly so that they can send their children to an independent school. Should they be allowed to do this?

Handicap

Mental and physical handicap can be doubly divisive. It can separate the handicapped persons themselves from the community, and also have serious effects on the family. There can be great tensions within the members of the family itself, but also between the family as a whole and outsiders. The family often feels guilt and embarrassment, as if they were to blame. Society at large often feels that there must be something wrong with people who have handicapped children and are reluctant to have much to do with them. Marriage into such a family, they say, is of course completely out of the question.

Has everyone an automatic right to the best that society has to offer? Should it depend to a certain extent on how much the individual is prepared to contribute to that society? Suggest other areas which tend to make divisions and inequality, and what can be done about them. Suggest other aspects of life which seem to make for inequality and divisions in society. Discuss what can be done to improve these.

WOMEN IN BRITISH SOCIETY

These are the traditional views of women in society that we see in cartoons and jokes. While all through history women have often been very powerful in private and in the home, it is true that in public, legally and politically, they have had very few rights until the last hundred years. The chart below shows some of the main laws which have tried to give women equality with men, but in spite of these, in practice if not in law, there are still differences.

Married Women's Property Act 1870. Until this Act was passed married women had no control over their own property or money. At marriage everything passed into the hands of their husbands who could do as they liked with it.

The Suffragette Movement 1903 -1914, led by Emmeline Pankhurst and her daughters, helped to get the Representation of the People Act 1917 passed. This gave women over 30 who were householders the right to vote for the first time in parliamentary elections.

Equal Pay Act 1970. This Act forces employers to pay women the same wages as men if they are doing the same, or a very similar job, or one which has been given an equal value by a job evaluation scheme.

1870 · 1875 · 1917 · 1921 · 1970 · 1975

University Enabling Act 1875. This Act allowed universities to grant degrees to women. The first woman doctor, Elizabeth Anderson qualified in Paris in 1871, but London University began medical courses for women doctors in 1877. The chance of higher education for even a few women did give a hope of higher status.

Representation of the People Act 1928. This gave all women over 21 the right to vote in parliamentary elections. This gave women complete political equality with men who had had the right to vote at 21 since 1884.

Sex Discrimination Act 1975. This Act makes it illegal for anyone to discriminate against women. They have to be treated the same as men in education, jobs, buying goods and services, and housing (including getting mortgages). It is illegal to discriminate between men and women in advertisements.

The number of married women working full time has risen steadily through the century.

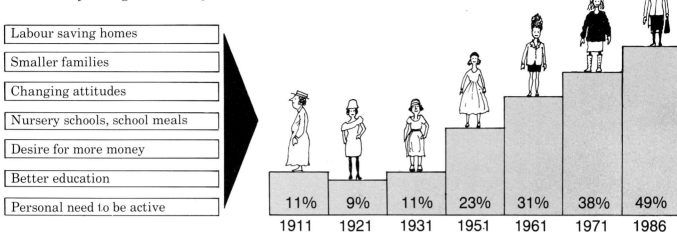

| Labour saving homes |
| Smaller families |
| Changing attitudes |
| Nursery schools, school meals |
| Desire for more money |
| Better education |
| Personal need to be active |

| 11% | 9% | 11% | 23% | 31% | 38% | 49% |
| 1911 | 1921 | 1931 | 1951 | 1961 | 1971 | 1986 |

In spite of the Equal Pay Act 1970 and the Sex Discrimination Act 1975, the average wages of employed women is about 75% that of men.

Women tend to get the more poorly-paid jobs such as repetitive factory work or employment based on domestic-type activities — cleaning, kitchen work etc. Part-time work which is done by about 40% of working women, tends to be simple, boring — and badly paid.

Although employment for married women has many advantages, there can be some social problems.

There may be some neglect of children especially when they are babies. Older children often have to come home from school to empty houses and fend for themselves.
With both partners living completely separate lives for most of the day, there may be strains on the marriage when they both come home tired after a hard day's work.

Employers are less likely to appoint women to long-term responsibility because they feel that they may leave to get married, have children, or move if their husband gets another job. A woman with a family is more likely to have time off when children are ill, or want hours which fit in with their needs.

With sexes working together there is more possibility of extra-marital relationships developing especially when the partners often see each other only in worst circumstances when both are tired after work.
Local social relationships — neighbours, relatives — may be poorer. Each family can become a small isolated unit with little contact with others in the same street or area.

In sexual or racial discrimination the law can go only so far, because people will usually find a way round it if they want to. As important as legislation are the changes in people's attitudes and the conditions under which they live. Two World Wars and rapid technological development have had an immense effect on the position of women in society today. In the nineteenth century the woman's place was the home, where she was completely in the hands of her husband. Yet marriage was the only goal of every girl's dreams. Not to be married and have a home and large family, was almost a disgrace. The wife had little to do except supervise the running of the home, and be a kind of ornament. Her own wishes had always to be subordinate to those of her husband.

Most people no longer consider marriage and a family to be the only goal for girls. Today it is accepted that some women may want to follow a career instead of getting married, or if they do marry to put the career before having children.

Labour-saving devices such as electrical equipment, ready-prepared and frozen foods, low-maintenance homes, synthetic materials, and hundreds of inventions that make life easier, mean that women do not have to spend long hours on housework. They have now a great deal of leisure, and would become bored if they did not have a job or outside interests.

Easy and reliable contraception, especially the pill and other devices used by the woman rather than the man, means that women can decide whether they want to become pregnant or not. If they do accidentally become pregnant legalised abortion is available. With these choices families are much smaller than in the past. This has meant that children can be better cared for and frees women for work or other activities.

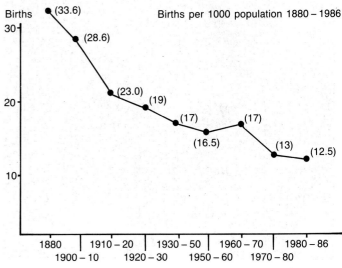

With rising expectations and living standards, couples want good houses with modern equipment such as furniture, fridges, washing machines, television as well as cars, leisure activities and holidays. This often means that both have to work, and bring new experiences and new interests as well as money into the home so that their lives are broader and freer.

The attitude of the public to working wives has changed. Once it was considered that the wife's place was at home, and those who went out to work were neglecting their 'duty' to husband and family. Today society realises that women need work, and work needs women, and provides facilities such as nursery schools and school meals for children of mothers who want jobs.

Boys and girls now have equal educational opportunities right to the highest level. In the past it was believed that girls did not need real education but today we realise that the better the education the better the person will be generally, whether at work, as a housewife, as a mother or as a partner.

The changing attitudes towards women, and the fact that women often contribute as much to the family budget as men, is altering the idea that the man is the master and the woman a kind of servant. Now many relationships are partnerships with both sharing domestic jobs, household repairs, DIY, and leisure activities. The sharing also extends to sexual relations, where women are no longer expected to be passive partners, but to take an active part in love-making. People living together without a formal marriage ceremony, and divorce when marriages break down are no longer considered sinful and socially unacceptable as they were until recently. This has made society much freer for women.

MIGRATION

International migration

Every year thousands of people come to, or leave, Britain. Many of them work in business or for other governments and will not stay for more than a year or two, but some do come to settle permanently. The chart below shows the numbers of people of different races who in 1984 were immigrants or emigrants.

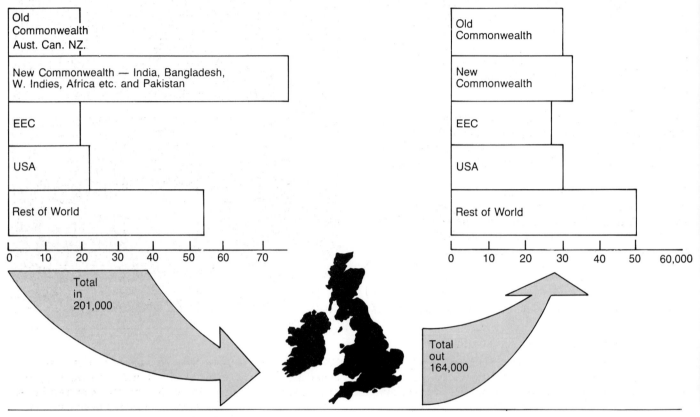

Internal migration

As well as people moving to and from other countries there is a steady movement of people from one part of the British Isles to another. Today this is mainly a drift from the midlands, the north, Wales, Scotland and Northern Ireland to London and the south-east region. There are, of course, many people who move *from* the south-east to other parts of the country, but except to the south-west and the east coast these are outnumbered by those coming in the other direction. The chart below shows the difference between the numbers of people moving to and from London and the south-east in 1984.

Net population movements 1984

56

Reasons for the drift to the south-east

1. Employment is the main reason. The northern counties, Wales, Scotland and Northern Ireland have traditionally depended on heavy industries such as coal, iron, steel and ship-building. These were produced often by old-fashioned methods, using large amounts of labour. Today, many of these products are no longer needed, or else they are made by much more efficient methods in countries such as Japan or Taiwan. In some cases British trade unions have not helped by restrictive practices. As a result the British industries have been forced to close, and few new ones have taken their places.

Unemployed steel worker

The chart below shows some of the reasons for the drift to the south-east. Suggest reasons for house prices being higher in the south-east, and the number of pupils staying at school after 16 being greater.

2. Many people think London and the south-east is a better place to live. Younger people especially think the entertainments, the shops and the social life is more exciting. Many business people find the south-east more convenient as it is near the 'centre of things' — head offices of firms are usually here; communications are better. Older people who are retiring often feel that the climate is better in the south-east in addition to the other social attractions.

Hitech female worker

Reasons for the drift from the south-east

1. The movement to the south-west is largely people moving to: (a) a better climate and countryside for retirement; (b) Bristol and Avon which are rapidly developing hi-tech industries, and many young technicians and professionals move there.

2. It is largely commuters who move to the east coast, as they can easily reach London to work by the new fast electrified railway. As the chart shows house prices here are for the moment much lower than in the south-east and attract people to move.

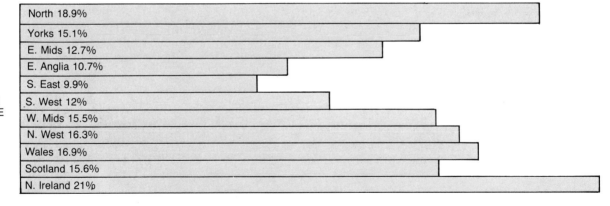

UNEMPLOYMENT — % OF WORK FORCE 1984

Region	%
North	18.9%
Yorks	15.1%
E. Mids	12.7%
E. Anglia	10.7%
S. East	9.9%
S. West	12%
W. Mids	15.5%
N. West	16.3%
Wales	16.9%
Scotland	15.6%
N. Ireland	21%

AVE. WEEKLY INCOME PER FAMILY 1984

North	£164
Yorks	£168
East Mids	£188
E. Anglia	£181
S. East	£231
S. West	£191
W. Mids	£180
N. West	£178
Wales	£165
Scotland	£176
N. Ireland	£153

Statistics

Presenting statistics

Statistics is collecting and presenting information through figures. This information can be absolutely essential in running a home, a business or a country as it enables people to plan ahead on the basis of what has happened in the past.

Statistics can be presented in a number of ways to suit the material and the people for which they are intended. They can also be manipulated to give a false impression, even though they are actually telling the truth. The British Prime Minister Benjamin Disraeli once said, 'There are three sorts of untruth — lies, damned lies . . . and statistics.'

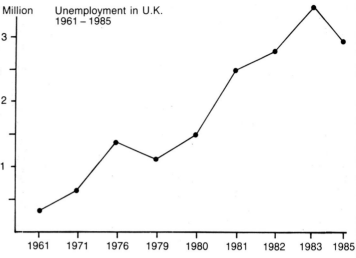

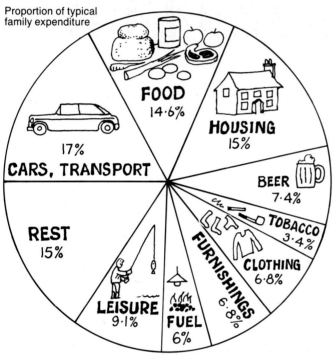

Proportion of typical family expenditure

Data with a single variable

These are the simplest forms of statistics. They can be such things as the number of unemployed over a number of years, or how a family divides up its income into rent, food etc., in a single year.

The simplest way of presenting such data is in a table. They can also be displayed as line graphs, and bar or pie charts.

What are the advantages and disadvantages of each of these forms of presentation? Which ones do you think would be most useful (1) for a serious student, (2) for a popular newpaper, and (3) to give an immediate impression of the trend?

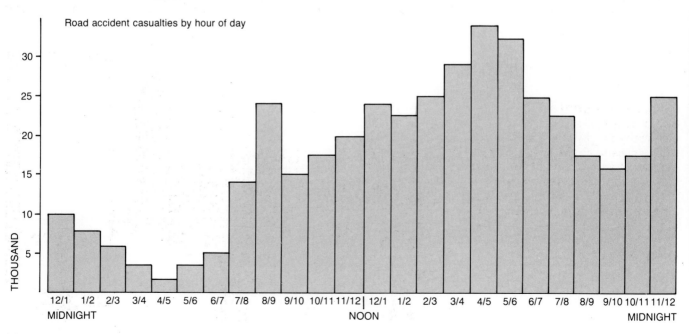

Data with two or more variables

Often we want to compare two or more lots of figures. This is usually done by tables, or by line graphs, though bar charts are sometimes used.

National Health Service — costs per person by age and sex, 1981.

Age	Males	Females
under 1	£473	£386
1 - 4	£178	£157
5 - 15	£111	£100
16 - 24	£114	£111
25 - 44	£126	£131
45 - 64	£193	£184
65 - 74	£407	£370
75 and over	£772	£947

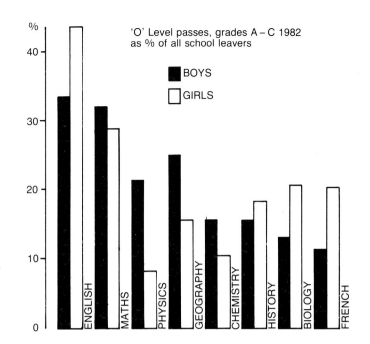

'O' Level passes, grades A – C 1982 as % of all school leavers

■ BOYS
□ GIRLS

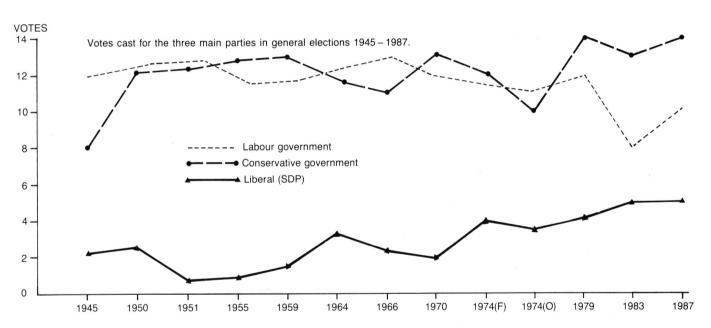

Votes cast for the three main parties in general elections 1945 – 1987.

- - - - Labour government
— ● — Conservative government
— ▲ — Liberal (SDP)

Pictorial presentation

Statistics are often presented pictorially for popular use. The chart opposite shows the average number of votes needed to elect one MP of each of the three main parties in the 1983 general election. Do you think this presentation adds anything to a simple bar chart? Or is this trying to influence us into a certain way of thinking?

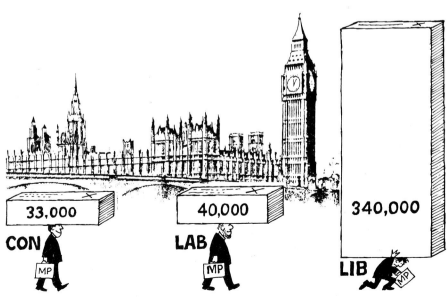

CON 33,000
LAB 40,000
LIB 340,000

SLANTING STATISTICS

Clever people can manipulate statistics to give just the impression they want. Because these are figures, which we say cannot lie, we tend to believe them. The figures are indeed generally correct but the way they are presented often leads us to assume something else unless we look very closely at them.

One of the easiest ways of distorting statistics is to adjust the scales to exaggerate the effect. The actual numbers of males convicted of serious offences per 1 000 of the population is 1961 - 11; 1967 - 13; 1972 - 19; 1977 - 21; 1982 - 22. Look how these two imaginary societies presented this data to justify their own cases. By altering the scales one gives the impression that the increase is worse than it is, and the other that it is less. Often these people will leave out the actual numbers (in this case on the vertical axis) so that the graph is even more exaggerated.

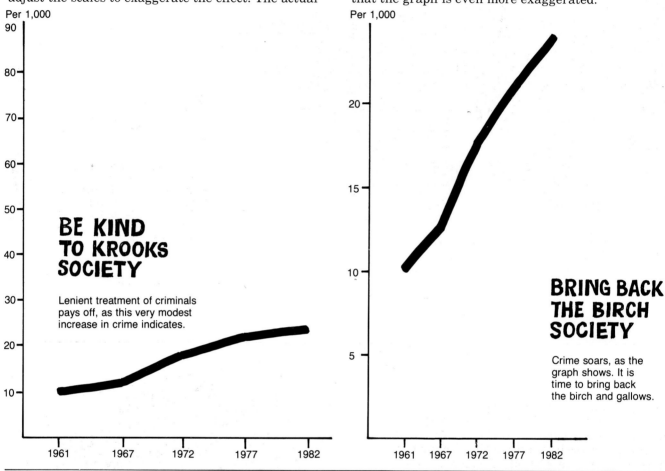

BE KIND TO KROOKS SOCIETY

Lenient treatment of criminals pays off, as this very modest increase in crime indicates.

BRING BACK THE BIRCH SOCIETY

Crime soars, as the graph shows. It is time to bring back the birch and gallows.

Another frequently-used trick is to magnify a part of the scale, and not to start it at zero. The impressive graph being displayed by the tricky chairman below actually shows an increase in turnover of £100 000 ... £100 100 ... £100 200, which because of inflation really means a fall.

THEREFORE, GENTLEMEN, IN VIEW OF THE EXCELLENT TRADING SHOWN IN THIS CHART, I RECOMMEND ALL DIRECTORS BE GIVEN A BONUS OF £10,000....

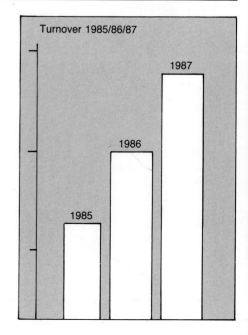

Turnover 1985/86/87

1985
1986
1987

Not giving the *whole* information can distort the effect of statistics. The serious crime convictions in the regions of Britain in 1982 (Scotland and Northern Ireland cannot be directly compared) show that London and the south-east have three times as many convictions as the next highest, Yorkshire and Humberside. But this chart does not tell us, as the official Home Office one did, that, worked out on the number of convictions per 1000 people over ten, London and the south-east is third in the table.

SERIOUS CRIME CONVICTIONS 1982

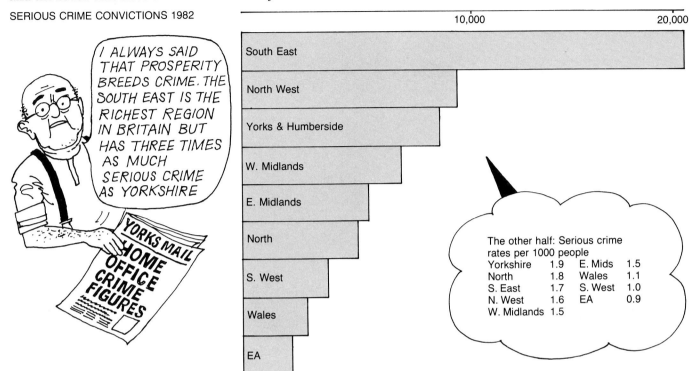

Selecting just those figures which suit the people involved can give a totally wrong impression — and would, in the case shown below, be illegal. Yet it is often done, if not so blatantly as this. Phake and Phoney, far from being 'stable' financially, are extremely unstable.

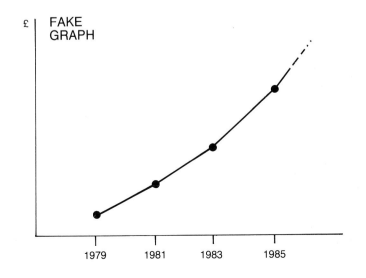

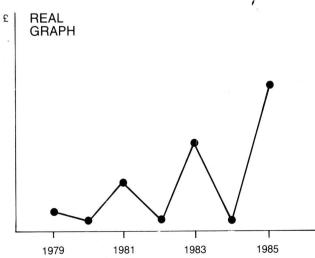

INTERPRETING STATISTICS

Statistics present us with the raw facts: it is up to us to find out what they mean and what the factors behind the figures are.

Look carefully at the statistics of deaths and serious injury on the roads in 1971 and 1984. Remember that the number of private vehicles rose from 13 million in 1971 to 18 million in 1984; the number of motorcycles rose from 1 million to 1.25 million; and goods vehicles fell from 7 million to 6 million. The number of motor cars rose by 36% but the accident rate fell by 26%. The number of motorcycles rose by 20%, but the number of serious accidents rose by 23%. Can you give possible reasons for (1) the general fall in serious accidents except for motor cyclists; (2) the dramatic fall in the number of motorists killed or seriously injured in spite of the increased numbers. Is this safe cars? Better driving? Better roads? Safety belts? Better policing? (3) Why should there be an increase in the number of serious motor cycle accidents? More powerful machines? Younger riders? Discuss other aspects of these figures.

Look carefully at the table showing what the 'average' household spent weekly in 1971 and 1981. The figures are all at 1981 prices to account for inflation. Discuss the major changes which took place, and try to give reasons for them.

Getting behind the statistics

Average weekly household expenditure (in £s, at 1981 prices)		
	1971	1982
Bread, biscuits, cake	4.7	3.5
Meat and bacon	7.8	6.7
Fish	1.1	0.9
Butter, margarine, fats	1.1	1.0
Milk, cheese, eggs	4.3	4.0
Sugar, jams, sweets etc	3.1	2.5
Vegetables	3.2	2.5
Alcoholic drink	6.8	10.0
Tobacco	6.8	4.5
Gas	1.2	2.3
Electricity	3.4	3.9
Household durables	5.3	8.2
Clothes, footwear	7.1	10.2
Transport, cars	16.3	19.2
Services	6.4	8.3
Food in cafés, hotels, pubs	6.1	5.3

Persons reporting chronic sickness: by sex and socio-economic group

[1] England and Wales only.
[2] Percentage reporting any long-standing illness, disability, or infirmity.

Source: General Household Survey 1972 1976 1982

Study the charts of people reporting chronic (i.e. long-standing) sickness for the years 1972, 1976 and 1982. They are divided into male and female, and socio-economic groups.

There are two very marked trends common to both sexes. What are these, and how do you account for them? Are women generally more unhealthy than men? Are unskilled workers generally more unhealthy than professional workers? Do working conditions have any effect on the figures? Does job-satisfaction play a part in not reporting sickness?

One of the problems with statistics is that there is often not a *single* reason for the figures, but a whole series of possible factors which are almost impossible to disentangle. People will often seize on just one of these to justify their case and not mention the others.

This is a graph of the deaths in Great Britain from all forms of cancer and from heart disease in the years 1953–82. Does it mean that cancer and heart disease are spreading like a plague?

Before we can really put the statistics into perspective we should also know:
1. How much the total population has increased in those years. The more people there are, the more are going to die in any year.

2. The age structure of the population: cancer and heart failure are generally diseases of elderly people. The more older people there are in a society, the higher the number of deaths there will be from cancer and heart conditions.

3. Have there been any changes in life style in those years — more alcohol, more smoking, change of diet (more fats and sugar, for example), more pollution from industry and transport, more stress from work and other situations can all help to cause these two diseases.

4. Better diagnosis. Doctors now have much better ways of finding out exactly what is wrong.

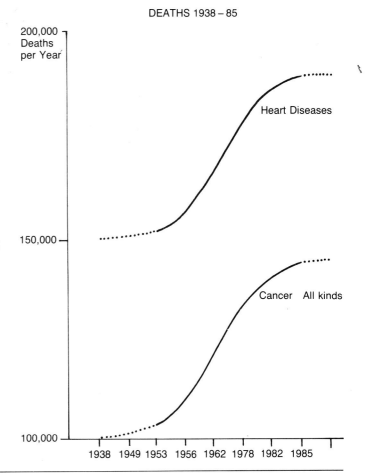

DEATHS 1938 – 85

School leavers with 3 or more GCE 'A' level passes
Academic year 1981/82

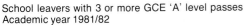

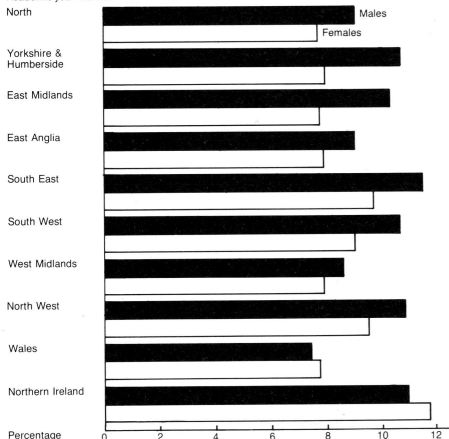

'A' Level passes
The bar charts shows the percentage of all school leavers in the different regions of Great Britain who gained three or more 'A' level passes.
What are the main *facts* we can learn from the graph — the proportions of male/female students gaining passes, the passes in the different regions, etc.
Suggest some possible reasons for these differences. What other information might you need to know to make a judgement?
Write a biased article, with a headline, for a newspaper based on these statistics. You can take such stands as: males are more intelligent than females; females are not given the opportunities; students for certain regions are duller/brighter than others.

Questions

Changing social patterns

1. Income and wealth

Selected Differences in Terms and Conditions of Employment.			
	Factory Workers	Clerical Workers	Senior Managers
Holidays: 15+ days per year	38%	74%	88%
Choice of holiday time	35%	76%	88%
Normal working hrs. 40+ per week	97%	9%	22%
Pay deductions for lateness	90%	8%	0%
No clocking on or signing in	2%	48%	94%
(% figures based on responses from 815 establishments)			

   (a) Which group of people work the greatest number of hours per week?

   (b) 74% of which group of people have more than 15 days holiday per year.

   (c) Looking at the chart as a whole, which group of people appear to have the best working conditions?

   (d) Write all you can about how class and jobs are linked and why different classes have different leisure activities.

2. Income and wealth

"People change jobs and sometimes this change involves a change of social class...."

   (a) What is 'social mobility'?

   (b) How is 'social mobility' measured?

   (c) Describe how a change in job *may* involve a change in social class.

   (d) Explain how a person can become *socially mobile* in Britain.

3. Income and wealth

Read the following paragraph and study the tables. Then answer the questions below.

All people have two kinds of resources. One we call wealth and is the things which we possess; the other is income and is what we have to spend at any one time. In this country there are great differences between the amount of wealth and income which people have.

Table 1: The distribution of wealth in the UK
Total population owning wealth

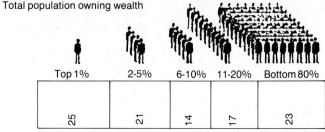

Top 1%	2-5%	6-10%	11-20%	Bottom 80%
25	21	14	17	23

Total wealth %

Table 2: The Distribution of Income in the UK before tax
Population divided into tenths

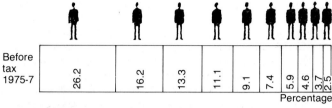

Before tax 1975-7	26.2	16.2	13.3	11.1	9.1	7.4	5.9	4.6	3.7	2.5

Percentage

Table 3: The Distribution of Income after tax

After tax 1975-7	23.2	16.0	13.3	11.2	9.3	7.7	6.6	6.1	4.5	3.0

Percentage

   (a) What is the difference between wealth and income?

   (b) How much of the nation's wealth do the wealthiest 1% of the population own?

   (c) What conclusions do you come to about the distribution of wealth in this country?

   (d) What is the main way in which the distribution of income is different to the distribution of wealth?

   (e) What difference does the payment of tax seem to make to the way in which income is distributed in this country?

   (f) Explain how the very rich come to have their wealth.

   (g) What causes some people to be much poorer than others?

4. Income and wealth

   (a) Read the following passage, then answer the questions below.

The National Income is the value of all the goods and services produced in the country in a year. If more goods and services are produced than in the past year, the economy is said to have 'grown'.

Most social scientists think that economic growth is good since people can now enjoy a higher standard of living than before, and the country can afford to spend more on such things as health and education.

Not all social scientists think that growth is good. Producing more goods and services can mean more pollution, a poorer living and working environment, etc. Growth creates problems.

     (i) What are 'goods' and 'services'? Give *one* example of each.

     (ii) Suggest *three* ways of measuring whether or not people have 'a higher standard of living' than in the past years.

     (iii) Why has the amount spent on health and education increased greatly over the last forty years?

   (b) Explain *two* ways by which Government can encourage economic growth.

   (c) Explain in detail the *problems* associated with economic growth.

5. Social inequality

Read the following passage and study the two tables. Then answer the questions below.

In every human society there is some form of social inequality. Class is one type of social stratification. Social stratification is a system in which groups are ranked, one above the other, usually in terms of wealth, power and prestige. There are many types of social stratification, based on different forms of social inequality.

Class is the main system of social stratification in Western industrial societies. There is no one way of defining social class. Some use occupation as the main sign of a person's class, but others consider wealth and income, or power as being the most important factor.

The following table gives an outline of the Registrar-General's classification of social class.

Table (1)   **THE REGISTRAR-GENERAL'S SOCIAL CLASSIFICATION**

Social Class	Examples of Occupations in Each Class
Class 1 Professional	Accountant, doctor, solicitor.
Class 2 Managerial and Technical	Manager, teacher, librarian, nurse.
Class 3 Skilled Manual	Electrician, printer, chef.
Class 4 Semi-Skilled Manual	Postman, shop assistant, telephone operator.
Class 5 Unskilled Manual	Labourer, cleaner, porter.

Table (2)   **RATES PER 1,000 REPORTING LONG STANDING ILLNESS BY SOCIAL CLASS 1972**

	1	2	3	4	5	All
Long-standing illness	130	168	192	192	265	206

(a) Explain what is meant by 'social stratification'.

(b) Which of the social classes listed in the Registrar-General's classification (Table 1) are usually called middle-class?

(c) What does the Registrar-General's classification use as the main sign of a person's class? What is a main advantage of using this as a sign of a person's class?

(d) What is the main conclusion which you make from Table 2 about the connection between social class and health?

(e) Describe *two other* differences between the lives of people in higher and lower social classes.

(f) Some people say that social class based on the Registrar-General's classification is no longer the best way of dividing people into social groups. Explain how such a statement could be justified.

6. Social inequality

(a) Explain what is meant by the terms:
(i) Absolute poverty
and (ii) Relative poverty

(b) Describe briefly how poverty in Britain today is different from poverty at the turn of the century.

(c) List the groups which are said to make up the majority of poor people in Britain.

(d) Examine some of the reasons for the persistence of poverty in Britain.

7. Social inequality

RACIAL DISADVANTAGE IN BRITAIN
EARNINGS

Median gross weekly earnings in 1974.	
White men	£40.20
All minority men	£36.70
West Indians	£37.70
Pakistanis/Bangladeshis	£35.40
Indians	£38.10
African Asians	£34.10

1968 RACE RELATIONS ACT

Made it unlawful to treat one person less favourably than another on grounds of colour, race or ethnic or national origin. The act covered employment, housing and the provision of goods, facilities and services.

1976 RACE RELATIONS ACT

Set up the Commission for Racial Equality, with much greater powers to enforce the provision against discrimination.

(a) Explain what is meant by racial discrimination in relation to employment.

(b) How do acts of Parliament such as the two shown above try to reduce racial discrimination?

(c) Why, in spite of these laws, is there still discrimination in employment?

(d) What problems do such inequalities sometimes cause in our society?

8. Women in British society

"Some of the most solidly researched and validated findings in the social sciences relate to the differential participation of men and women in political activities.... Women have been found to vote less than men, to participate in political parties less than men, to know less about politics than men, to have less interest in politics than men and to be more conservative than men."

R Dowse and J A Hughes
'Girls, Boys and Politics'

(a) As a social scientist how would you explain this situation?

(b) What evidence is there that women are becoming more 'political' than the extract suggests?

9. Women in British society

WOMEN IN UNIONS

While women are still not as strongly unionised as men, the proportion of women members in unions has been slowly growing, so that while in 1930 only about 1 in 8 TUC members were women, by 1975 this figure had risen to 1 in 4.

In particular unions, women account for a very high percentage of total union membership. In traditional 'women's industries' this has long been the case; for example in the Tailor and Garment Workers' Union and the National Union of Hosiery and Knitwear Workers, women account for about three quarters of the total membership. The same is true in the National

Union of Teachers. But more recently there has been a rapid expansion of women's membership in the general and public service unions;

For example: in NUPE the percentage of women
members has risen from 24% in
1950 to 62% in 1974.
in COHSE the percentage of women
members rose from 38% in 1950 to
67% in 1974.

The expansion of public service unions is mainly due to rising membership among women. And it is this expansion that has helped keep up overall trade union membership in this country, as traditional industries have declined.

(a) What is meant by the term "women's industries"?

(b) Which are the *two* general and public service unions mentioned in the text?

(c) Name *four* occupations which have a high percentage of women employees.

(d) Give *five* reasons why more women work today than ever before.

10. Women in British society

EMOTIONAL   TIMID   GIVEN TO PANIC

A GOSSIP

UNABLE TO KEEP A SECRET

NO SENSE OF HUMOUR   ENJOYS BEING MASTERED   CATTY

(a) What does 'stereotype' mean?

(b) Give one other example of a stereotype applied to women.

(c) Why do you think men view women in the ways shown by the above?

(d) From your Social Studies work, describe some of the ways in which women are discriminated against.

11. Women in British society

Working Wives and Mothers:

The pattern today is to work until marriage, work after marriage until children arrive and return to work when children grow older. Marriage and a family no longer mean an end to paid employment for women, but simply an interruption.

(a) Give three reasons why some mothers may return to work.

(b) Give *two* reasons why some mothers do not return to work.

(c) Why has the number of married women working increased.

(d) Write a paragraph on facilites available to help working mothers. How could these be improved.

12. Population

BIRTH RATE PER 1000 POPULATION
U.K. 1951 – 1975

1951	15.8
1961	17.9
1966	18.0
1971	16.2
1972	14.9
1975	12.4

(a) By how much has the birth rate fallen between 1951 and 1975?

(b) Give *one* reason why the birth rate rose in the early 1960s.

(c) Explain what is meant by the following terms:
i) Crude Birth Rate; ii) Crude Death Rate.

(d) Suggest *four* reasons why families today tend to have fewer children than families 100 years ago.

13. Population

Examine the information in the table and extracts below, then answer the questions which follow.

Balance of the Sexes
"A third factor in changing population trends is the balance of the sexes at different age levels. For much of this century there have been more women than men at almost all ages. At present there is a majority of men in the under fifteen group, and this is likely to grow between now and the end of the century. In the fifteen to sixty-four age range there are at present more women than men but by 2001 this will have been reversed. For every thousand women in 1931 there were only 905 men. By 1965 there were 997 men and by the end of the century there are likely to be 1031 men to every 1000 women. Women will always be in the majority in the upper age groups. Even by 2001 there will only be 710 men per thousand women over sixty-five and over eighty there will be little more than

300. The balance of the sexes has important implications for the rate of marriage in any one age group. On average women marry men who are three years older than themselves. Thus the bulge in the birth rate in 1947 created a situation where there were not enough men three years older to provide partners for the 'bulge' women and not enough women three years younger to provide for the 'bulge' men. This created imbalance in the proportion of the population who are married in these generations."

Source: "People in Society", P.J. North-Longmans.

Age distribution of United Kingdom population 1901 – 2001

	Percentage of the total population					
	1901	*1911*	*1931*	*1951*	*1961*	*2001 (projected)*
Age group	*%*	*%*	*%*	*%*	*%*	*%*
Under 15	32.4	30.9	24.2	22.5	23.4	28.1
15 – 64	62.8	63.9	68.4	66.5	63.9	60.5
65 and over	4.8	5.2	7.4	11.0	11.7	11.4
	100	100	100	100	100	100

Source: The Registrar-General

(a) (i) In which year was the under 15 age group at its least as a proportion of the total population?

(ii) What percentage of the population was aged below 65 in 1961?

(iii) In which year was the over 65 age group at its greatest as a proportion of the total population?

(b) State what happened to the birth-rate in 1947 and using the evidence from Extract 2, explain in your own words what effect this had on marriage for the people of ths and other generations.

(c) Describe the trend in the proportion of the population in Britain which was 65 and over between 1981 and 1961; and suggest reasons for this trend.

(d) "By 2001 there will have been a growth in the proportion of people aged under 15 and an increasing proportion of women in the 15-64 age group." Quote figures from the evidence to assess the accuracy of this statement.

(e) How might government spending change because of an ageing population?

14. Statistics

Choose *three* of the following methods of data collection:

structured interview	participant observation
mail questionnaire	secondary sources
experiment	(documents, diaries etc)
	unstructured interview.

(a) Show, with examples, how social scientists use each of the methods.

(b) Discuss the strength and weaknesses of the methods you have chosen.

15. Statistics

(a) What is meant by a random sample and why are random samples important in social survey work?

(b) Briefly explain the meaning of *three* of the following terms:

the mode	standard deviation
the mean	the normal distribution
the median	correlation.

16. Statistics

The following questions are taken from a research survey which investigated people's opinions and attitudes regarding different types of shops. Take each question in turn, and state, briefly, whether the question is appropriate and comment on any aspects of the question you regard as being poorly constructed.

Shopping Survey

(a) What is your age? −20 ☐ 20-30 ☐ 30-40 ☐ 40-50 ☐ 50-60 ☐ 60-70 ☐ 70+ ☐

(b) Have you any dependent children? Yes/No
If yes, how many?.............

(c) How long have you lived in this district?
..........years.

(d) What social class would you say you were?
working class ..... lower-middle class ......
middle class....... upper-middle class ......

(e) Do you consider shopping to be a tedious necessity? Yes/No/Don't know

(f) Do you feel goods are likely to be fresher in a self-service shop because of a higher turnover? Yes/No/Don't know

(g) Do you think of the self-service shop as something large and impersonal and not really requiring the loyalty that would be afforded to a small grocer whom you know? Yes/No/Don't know

(h) Do you agree with the following statements?
(i) Self-service shops are cheap, efficient and clean.
Yes/No
(ii) Assistants in counter-service shops are always more helpful and efficient than in self-service shops.
Yes/No

17. Statistics

One of the major problems in social research is getting respondents to say what they really think. Discuss the extent to which each of the following methods tries to solve the problem.

(a) observation

(b) postal questionnaires

(c) open-ended interviews

18. Statistics

You are in charge of a team of interviewers appointed to investigate the needs of old people living alone in your own area. Your interviewers are men and women aged between 20 and 50.

Write a document giving advice to your interviewers. Use no more than 250 words in your answer.

The nature of politics

POLITICAL SYSTEMS

A - - - - - B

Even the simplest operation, such as going from A to B, can be done in many ways, depending on the circumstances — distance, cost, time and so on. Running a country is infinitely more complicated, and it is not surprising that everyone has his or her way of thinking how this can be done best. Today, however, most ideas fall into one of two main groups, which we can call Left and Right.

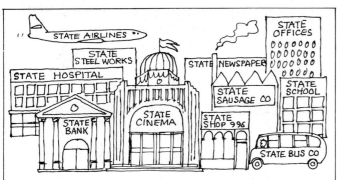

Left
The State should own everything — factories, land, mines, transport, banks, commerce, shops, education, medical care, welfare and even entertainment. It will operate all of these for the benefit of everyone. Naturally everyone is employed by the State.

The State controls most aspects of life for everyone's benefit. People are sent to the job or place where the State thinks they are needed. There is strict control on travelling, especially abroad. Wages are fixed according to the needs of the country so that powerful groups of workers cannot get more than they deserve by striking. This means that everyone get a fairer share of the wealth that is available.

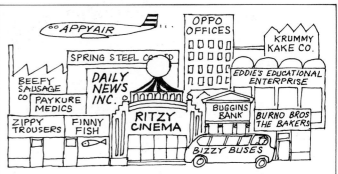

Right
Everything belongs to individual people or groups of people (free enterprise) who operate them for their own profit. They employ other people to work for them, and have to compete with others doing the same. Everyone is free to get what they can, or want, from the system.

There is complete freedom for everyone to do as they please as long as it is legal. People can take what jobs they like — or can get — live and travel where they like. They can go into the jobs where they think they will get the best wages, or strike for more money. Personal freedom is always a good thing, but sometimes it means the strong and clever can exploit the weak and less able. This means that there can be more inequality — rich and poor, privileged and under-privileged.

A centrally-planned economy

The State decides how much of everything — cars, coal, carpets and cabbages — will be needed and plans for just that amount to be produced in its own factories and farms. In this way there should be no wasteful surpluses, and no shortages — just enough for the country. Prices can be kept steady because there is no over- or under-production. There will be no different competing brands as everything will be 'State' brand.

Market, or capitalist, economy

Everything is produced by free enterprise — private firms competing with one another. Prices and supplies are regulated by the supply-and-demand principle. If not enough is produced, prices rise, and other firms make that product until there is enough and the price falls. If too much is produced, prices fall and firms stop producing or go out of business. Production and prices go up and down until a balance is reached — reasonable profit for the makers and sellers, reasonable price for the buyers.

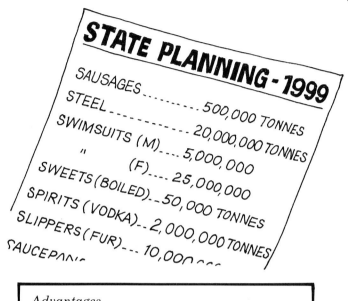

FIRMS STOP MAKING OR GO OUT OF BUSINESS

MORE FIRMS MAKE GOODS TO GET PROFITS

Advantages
1. No shortages or over production — prices can be kept steady at a level everyone can afford.
2. No wasteful duplication of different firms making similar goods in competition. Fewer different models and styles mean cheaper production costs and prices.
3. The whole economy can be planned for the benefit of everyone. Profits go to the State and not to make a few people very rich.

Disadvantages
1. The very complicated bureaucracy needed to plan the whole economy breaks down and inefficiency, shortages and poor quality result. The planners are generally civil servants who know little about the products.
2. There is little or no choice of models, and a very limited range of goods of all kinds. No competition means there is no incentive to improve the quality.
3. The State can fix the price at what it likes as there is no competition to force the price down.

CENTRALLY PLANNED ECONOMY

Advantages
1. Competition means a very wide range of goods of different types and prices to suit everyone.
2. Competition stimulates improvements — every firm tries to make better or cheaper goods than its rivals to get more trade.
3. The profit motive stimulates new ideas — new products and machines are always being introduced to make life easier and better.
4. The wide range of goods available encourages people to work harder to get a higher standard of living.

Disadvantages
1. As profit is involved manufacturers and sellers tempt people to buy more than they need or can afford, or else sell inferior goods.
2. Free enterprise can lead to dishonesty as people try to make money by illegal methods.
3. Competition means advertising, encouraging people to over-spend. The cost of advertising is merely added to the cost of the goods.
4. The wide range of goods emphasises the inequalities in society — some people can afford to ride in Rolls Royces, others have old bicycles.

CAPITAL OR MARKET ECONOMY

Central and local government

MONARCHY AND GOVERNMENT

The Monarch — king or queen — is a focus for the nation. It symbolises the whole State at home and in foreign affairs. The British monarchy is hereditary — that is, it passes from father to son, and to daughters if there are no male heirs. Because the monarchy passes in a direct line in one family it does not involve any political or factional problems. An elected or appointed head of state is usually an important political figure: a monarch is considered to be beyond both law and politics.

The monarch is head of all aspects of the State — the law, government, and the armed forces, and is the 'supreme governor' of the Church of England. The real power is of course in the hands of the Government of the day, but the monarch officially summons and dismisses Parliament, and appoints all ministers; declares war on and makes peace with other nations; invites and receives heads of foreign states. The monarch also appoints judges, senior officers of the forces, diplomats, bishops, peers and knights, and the Prime Minister; gives the Royal Assent to all laws, and pardons people convicted of crimes if necessary. All of these are done on the advice of government ministers.

The monarch also has important ceremonial duties, such as opening Parliament, visits to different parts of Britain, the Commonwealth and foreign countries; attendance at great national occasions such as Remembrance Day and other services, and giving out awards, decorations and honours such as knighthoods and peerages.

The monarch also calls meetings of the Privy Council — a committee of 370 people, including all the members of the cabinet and important people from the Commonwealth. The monarch does not attend the many sub-committees of the Privy Council, but only the full Council, which meets only when a monarch dies or announces an intention to marry.

One of the most important duties of the sovereign is to invite a politician to become Prime Minister. This is normally the leader of the majority party in Parliament, but in the event of a resignation, the appointment is more difficult. But whatever the circumstances, the monarch must always be completely politically impartial.

The sovereign is the head of the State. The Government, and its senior officials, is nominally appointed by the monarch, who must approve everything it does (laws, declarations of war, etc). In practice the actions of the Government and Parliament are approved automatically, but the sovereign, with the most senior advisers in the Privy Council, can use some independence in the choice of Prime Minister, though rarely does so.

The Government consists of the Prime Minister, the Cabinet, and ministers outside the Cabinet. The Prime Minister is chosen by the sovereign, but is normally the leader of the majority party in Parliament, though he or she need not necessarily be a MP. The Prime Minister takes the chair at cabinet meetings, keeps the sovereign informed on what the Government is doing, and advises him or her on senior appointments.

The Cabinet consists of about 20 of the Prime Minister's senior colleagues who are in charge of different departments of government — defence, finance, home affairs etc. They are chosen, or dismissed, by the Prime Minister, with the approval of the sovereign. The Cabinet works out government policy, runs the country, and tries to get the different departments to work together. There are also a number of ministers who are not in the Cabinet (Attorney-General, housing, consumer affairs, etc). Ministers, who are likely to change every few years even if the same Government stays in power, cannot be expected to understand the complex problems of their departments, and are advised by their senior civil servants (see p.72). The Civil Service also sees that the decisions of the Government, when approved by Parliament and the sovereign, are carried out.

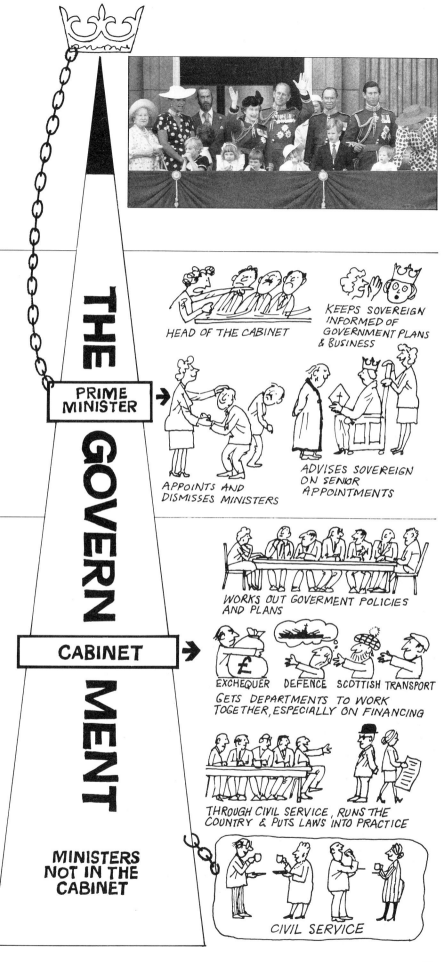

THE GOVERNMENT

PRIME MINISTER

HEAD OF THE CABINET

KEEPS SOVEREIGN INFORMED OF GOVERNMENT PLANS & BUSINESS

APPOINTS AND DISMISSES MINISTERS

ADVISES SOVEREIGN ON SENIOR APPOINTMENTS

CABINET

WORKS OUT GOVERMENT POLICIES AND PLANS

EXCHEQUER DEFENCE SCOTTISH TRANSPORT

GETS DEPARTMENTS TO WORK TOGETHER, ESPECIALLY ON FINANCING

THROUGH CIVIL SERVICE, RUNS THE COUNTRY & PUTS LAWS INTO PRACTICE

MINISTERS NOT IN THE CABINET

CIVIL SERVICE

GOVERNMENT DEPARTMENTS

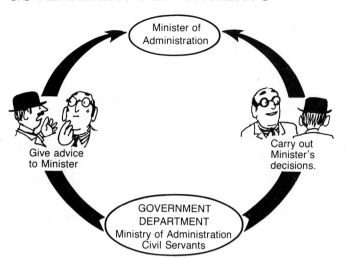

Government departments are units of the Civil Service which advise a particular minister, and put the decisions made by the Government into practice. In carrying out new legislation the Government departments may work directly, or through local authorities or other organisations. The Home Office for example makes the different constabularies carry out new police procedures: the Department of the Environment makes local authorities carry out pollution and conservation legislation.

Government departments are normally permanent, and do not change when another Government or minister comes into office. Most ministers have a single department, but some departments which do similar work have the same minister. The Treasury Ministers, for example, also run the Customs and Excise, Inland Revenue and National Savings.

Each Government department is funded separately by the Government through the Treasury, so that each minister has to fight if s/he thinks his/her department needs more money than has been allowed. This is particularly obvious in the departments such as Defence, Health, and Education which spend huge sums of money.

The main departments are: the Treasury; the Home Office; the Foreign and Commonwealth Office; Defence; Health and Social Security; Environment; Agriculture, Fisheries and Food; Industry; Education.

Quangos: (QUasi Autonomous Non Governmental Organisations) are set up by Governments for a specific purpose. There are at least 500 of them, and most consist of a committee of part- or full-time members with some full-time employees. There are three main types:

Executive: these have the power to spend money and employ staff. Examples are the Arts Council and the University Grants Committee.

Advisory: committees of experts and interested parties who collect information and do research in order to advise a minister before s/he begins new legislation or makes decisions.

Tribunals: these vary tremendously — they can be to resolve disputes, to set rents or social security payments, or to work on industrial problems. There are various ways of appealing from their decisions.

CIVIL SERVICE

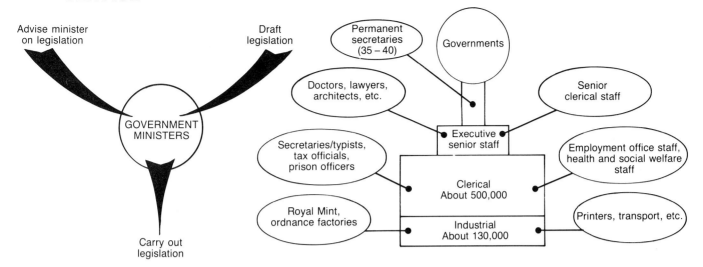

The work of government would be impossible without the civil service. The most senior civil servants advise the minister in charge of their department, draft new legislation and work out how it will be put into practice. Behind these very powerful top civil servants are over 600 000 men and women who: do clerical and secretarial work; run staff employment, social welfare, and tax offices; run the prison service; inspect schools; and run organisations such as the national museums and records and statistical offices.

Supporting the clerical and administrative staff are the industrial civil servants — people who make weapons for the Ministry of Defence, transport workers, employees of the Royal Mint and printers at the Stationery Office.

At the top of the Civil Service are the Permanent Secretaries of each Government department. They remain in their job whichever party is in power and so have to work very closely with Labour and Conservative ministers in turn. They are above party politics, and treat all ministers alike. Because of their experience and their knowledge of what has happened before they are extremely powerful. Ministers, who will have only a few years at most in that office, have to listen very carefully to their advice, and would normally be very foolish to ignore it. Much of the actual running of the country depends on the 35-40 Permanent Secretaries.

Disadvantages
1. The top people all come from the same narrow background.
2. They can manipulate the minister.
3. They do not like change or new ideas.
4. They keep everything too secret.
5. The departments often do not work together.

Advantages
1. There is virtually no corruption.
2. Personal or political attitudes do not influence advice given to ministers.
3. When necessary the Civil Service works quickly and efficiently.

The Civil Service balance

PARLIAMENT

Parliament is made up of three parts — the sovereign, the House of Lords and the House of Commons. The only time the three meet is at the State opening of Parliament: at all other times they work separately. Parliament has three main jobs: (1) To make new laws or repeal old ones; (2) To raise money from taxation to run the country; (3) To influence the Government's policies.

The House of Lords
The House of Lords is made up of about 1 200 peers, of whom about 300 attend the house each day. Although there is a permanent Conservative majority in the Lords, the peers do not keep so strictly to the party line as the Commons. The 'chairman' of the House of Lords is the Lord Chancellor, a lawyer, who sits on the Woolsack. Peers are of two types: hereditary and life.

ORDINARY LIFE PEERS

LAW LORDS

ARCHBISHOPS AND BISHOPS

HEREDITARY PEERS

Life peers
People who have been important in public life — ex-ministers, trade union leaders, etc. — are sometimes given peerages in the Honours Lists. Two archbishops and 24 senior bishops are members of the House of Lords.
9 law lords (senior judges) and any retired law lords are automatically life peers. They take part in ordinary business of the house, but more importantly they sit as the highest court of appeal in the country.

Hereditary peers
These are the heads of families which were given peerages in the past — some well over 400 years ago.

Normally the House of Lords cannot stop bills passed by the House of Commons — it can only delay them by making amendments and sending them back.
The only time the Lords can veto a bill outright is if the Commons attempts to prolong its own life for more than five years.

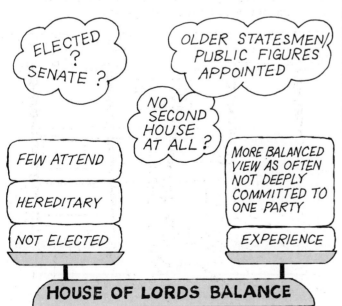

ELECTED? SENATE?

OLDER STATESMEN/ PUBLIC FIGURES APPOINTED

NO SECOND HOUSE AT ALL?

FEW ATTEND

HEREDITARY

NOT ELECTED

MORE BALANCED VIEW AS OFTEN NOT DEEPLY COMMITTED TO ONE PARTY

EXPERIENCE

HOUSE OF LORDS BALANCE

Today some people wonder whether the House of Lords should be abolished or changed: should a few hundred people have an important say in running the country just because their ancestors, perhaps hundreds of years ago, did something — or paid — to become peers? Should a second 'House' be elected as in the United States Senate, or should it be made up of all life peers, chosen for their known ability and experience in politics?

The House of Commons

The House of Commons is made up of 650 elected MPs, who are directly responsible to the electors. There must be a general election at least every 5 years, though the average length of Parliament since 1945 has been less than 3½ years. Parliament is dissolved by the sovereign on the advice of the Prime Minister, who can choose a time for a new election which he or she thinks will be best for the party in power at the time.

Parliament meets each year for a 'session' of about 175 days. Each session is opened by the sovereign at a ceremony in the House of Lords with both houses present. At this ceremony the sovereign reads the queen's/king's Speech, which is written by the Prime Minister, and sets out what legislation the Government hopes to deal with in that session.

Since 1911 MPs have been paid a salary (in 1986 this was £22 548 a year). In addition they can claim allowances for lodging, secretaries and other assistants up to £20 140 a year, plus travelling cost on parliamentary business. Ministers are paid much more: the Prime Minister gets £62 699, a Cabinet Minister £51 068 and the leader of the opposition £48 148, all plus expenses.

The party in government sit on the Speaker's right, and the Opposition on his left. Members of other parties are said to sit on the cross benches, though in practice there are none, and they sit on the same side as the Opposition. Ministers and more important members of the party sit on the seats nearer the Speaker, which are known as the front bench: ordinary MPs sit behind them on the back benches. The same arrangement applies to the Opposition — the Shadow Cabinet and Shadow Ministers sitting on the Opposition front bench, and the ordinary MPs on the Opposition back benches.

The Chairman of the House of Commons is the Speaker, who is elected by MPs from one of their colleagues. The Speaker is a lawyer, and once he (so far there have been no female speakers) is elected he takes no further part in the political side of debates, and cannot vote in divisions. His job is to rule the House as fairly and impartially as he can, keeping the House in order, deciding which MP shall speak or stop speaking, and ruling whether any member's comments can be allowed or not. He can order any members who persistently disobey the rules to leave the House, or even suspend them for a certain period.

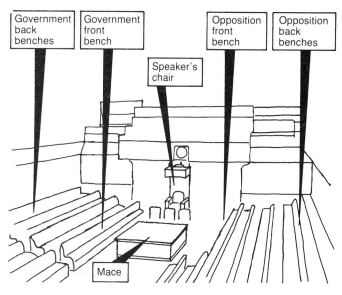

LEGISLATION

Almost all legislation is introduced by the Government, and never by the Opposition. In every session of Parliament, however, 20 back-benchers, selected by ballot, can introduce a 'Private members' Bill' on the twelve Fridays reserved for these.

Before introducing a bill the Government discusses it with pressure groups and interested parties. Then it is given its first reading in Parliament, when the broad ideas are debated.

If the general ideas are passed by Parliament, the bill is later given its second reading, when it is debated in more detail. If it passes this, it goes to...

the committee stage. A standing committee of 20-50 MPs of all parties discusses the bill in great detail, clause by clause, and makes any changes it thinks necessary. On very important bills the whole House of Commons may make itself the committee and discuss the legislation in detail.

The bill is re-submitted to Parliament for the report stage, when further amendments can be made.

At the third reading the bill is given in its final form, and is often voted on without any more debate.

It now goes to the House of Lords, where it goes through much the same procedure as the House of Commons. The Lords looks carefully at the legislation and may make some alterations, but usually only in small detail. The Lords can delay a bill for up to 13 months, but rarely does so.

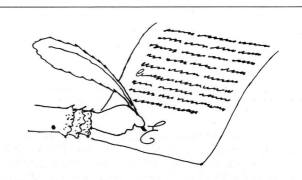

The bill now is sent to the Queen for signature, after which it becomes the law of the land. No monarch has refused to sign a bill since 1707.

◀ After the practical details have been worked out by the appropriate branch of the Civil Service, the legislation is put into force.

POLITICAL PARTIES

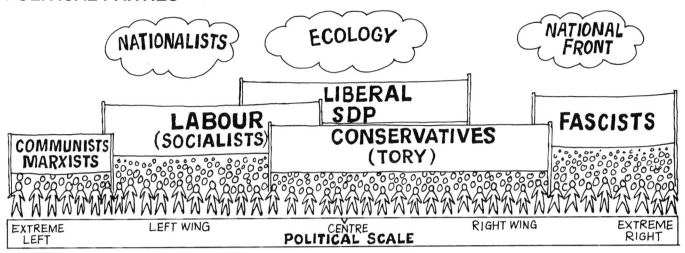

In parliamentary elections in Britain the majority of electors vote for the political party rather than for the actual candidate. They like that party's ideas and know that the candidate, if elected will, except in the most unusual circumstances, vote in Parliament for those policies. In Britain there are two main parties, Conservative and Labour, with a third, the Liberal/SDP Alliance, increasing in strength. There are many minor parties such as the Welsh and Scottish Nationalists, and the Northern Ireland parties, all of whom may have a few seats, and some such as the

Ecology Party and the National Front, who seem unlikely ever to have enough support in one place to get a single member.

The parties stretch from extreme Left (Communist) to extreme Right (Fascist), but inside each of the main parties there are wide differences — there are Left and Right-wing Labour supporters, and Right and Left-wing Conservatives. Today the main parties have much in common, but there are differences of emphasis.

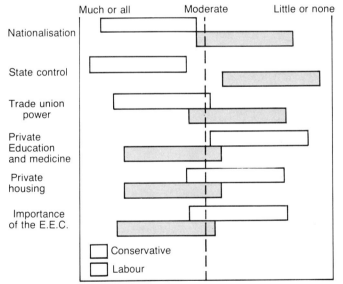

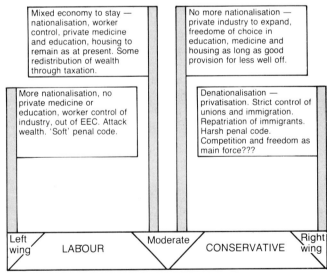

After a general election the leader of the majority party is normally asked to form a Government. The second largest party becomes the official Opposition, and its leader forms a Shadow Cabinet, with Shadow Ministers matching the Cabinet. The smaller parties support the Government or the opposition according to their views on any particular subject.

All parties appoint 'whips', MPs whose job it is to organise party business in the House, and to make sure that members of the party attend important votes (Divisions). Chief whips give their MPs summons to be present marked with one line (a one-line whip —

'attend if you can'), two-lines ('you must attend if possible'), and three-lines ('you *must* be present, even if it means, literally, coming by ambulance').

ELECTORAL SYSTEM

1970 ELECTION

This system can give strange results: the figures for the 1987 election are typical.

	Votes	MPs	Votes per MP
Conservative	13 738 899	375	36 637
Labour	10 033 633	229	43 815
Liberal/SDP	7 339 909	22	333 632

Conservatives with 45% of the votes won 61% of the seats: Labour with 29% of the votes had 32% of the seats, while the Liberal/SDP had 27% of the votes but only 3.5% of the seats. In other elections the Conservative/Labour situation is reversed: the winning party always gets its seats more 'cheaply', and the first-past-the-post system is particularly unfair to smaller parties who may get a fair number of votes throughout the country but no MPs at all.

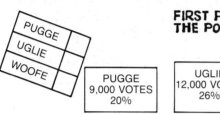

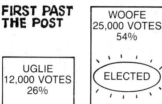

Proportional representation

Many people think that the number of MPs should bear a direct relationship to the total number of votes cast for any party. This is called proportional representation. If MPs had been shared out equally according to votes cast in the 1979 election the results would have been:

MPs: Conservative 299, Labour 251, Liberal/SDP 94.

Most countries of Europe have proportional representation: the one that some suggest should be adopted in Britain is the Alternative Vote. Instead of marking the ballot paper with a single cross the voters list the candidates in order of preference, 1st, 2nd, 3rd. The votes are counted as usual using the 1st choices only. If one candidate gets over 50% he or she is elected. If no one gets more than half the votes, the candidate with the lowest number is eliminated and their votes are distributed on the basis of second choice. If there are more than three candidates this may have to be done again until one emerges with more than 50% of the poll.

Proportional representation would probably still give the two present major parties the majority of MPs, but they would also probably be much more equal in number. It would also give the smaller parties considerably more seats. In normal circumstances neither of the two largest parties would have an overall majority — that is, more MPs than the others put together. This means that if the opposition parties all decided to vote together they could always defeat the Government.

To form a strong Government a major party would have to take one or more of the smaller parties into partnership either by agreeing to make some of the laws which the smaller party wanted, or by offering some of its MPs Cabinet posts. A Government formed by two parties together is called a coalition. Its weakness is that the smaller party, supported by a relatively small number of people compared with the larger ones, can hold the balance of power. By threatening to withdraw from the coalition and vote with the opposition it can sometimes make the Government take steps which the Government does not really want to take. Its strength is that the Government will not pass extreme laws which would upset its coalition partners in case they withdrew support. This means a much more moderate government — sometimes so much so that little gets done.

General elections

In Britain general elections for Parliament must be held at least every five years. The country is divided into 650 constituencies of about 40 000 - 80 000 electors. Each constituency sends one MP to Parliament. Everyone over the age of 18 can vote except members of the House of Lords, people serving a sentence in prison, and anyone who has been convicted of certain election frauds in the previous five years. Until recently Britain was very largely a two-party political system — Labour and Conservative. The other parties such as Liberals, Nationalists and Communists have been very small, with only a few MPs or none at all. The rise of the Liberal/SDP Alliance in the last few years may have changed this.

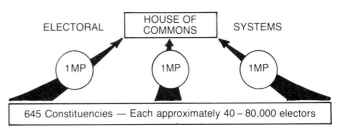

Each of the two main parties could on the whole rely on 10 or 11 million voters who would support them whatever happened, and elections are largely decided by the 'floating' or uncommitted voters. These are people who vote for the party which they think will be best in the circumstances at the time — they may vote Conservative at one election, Labour at the next, and Liberal at the one after.

When an election is announced people who wish to become candidates must get ten voters in that constituency to nominate them and then pay a deposit of £500 which they lose if they do not get 5% of the votes cast. The candidates then begin campaigning, holding meetings, touring the streets and giving out leaflets. To prevent rich people having an advantage no candidate must spend more on the campaign than £3 240 plus 3.4p for each voter in that constituency.

Voting is by secret ballot at a number of polling stations in each constituency. Voters have cards with their electoral numbers and these are checked against a complete list, so that people cannot vote twice. At the end of polling the sealed ballot boxes are taken to a central hall where the votes are counted. Where a result seems very close the candidates can demand a recount.

The member is elected by the first-past-the-post system — that is, the candidate who gets the largest number of votes wins. While this may seem reasonably fair, it is in theory possible to get a result like this:

A Toffe (Conservative)	15 002
P Snodge (Labour)	15 001
R Gruntle (Liberal/SDP)	15 000

Toffe is elected MP, even though two thirds of the electorate voted *against* him. It means in effect that from a party point of view the votes for the Labour and Liberal/SDP candidate were wasted.

NATIONAL GOVERNMENT FINANCE

In 1986/7 the British Government spent about
£165 000 000 000, or just under £3 000 for every person,
adult or child, in the country. If this were in £5 notes
placed end to end it would reach about 72 times round
the equator. This vast sum is spent on such things as
social security, defence, education, health as well as
many other services to the country. The Government
gets the money from the public by (1) taxes, and (2)
borrowing.

The Budget

The Treasury has to estimate each year how much
money the country will need for the following twelve
months and then work out how this can be raised. The
final decisions on this are made by the Chancellor of
the Exchequer with the advice of his senior civil
servants at the Treasury. The collection and spending
of the nation's money is so important that the Prime
Minister is always First Lord of the Treasury as well.
When the Chancellor, with his officials, has worked out
the details of the expenditure and the revenue for the
following year, he tells Parliament in his Budget
speech, which takes place normally in March or April.
He explains how he has 'balanced the Budget' — that
is, he tells them how much the country expects to spend
in the coming year, and how he proposes to get this
money through taxation or other means. If he thinks

that the nation will not be spending so much, he can
reduce taxes: if it will be spending more, then he must
increase taxes or bring in new ones.

Occasionally a Chancellor will make tax changes for
social reasons. For example, to try to reduce the danger
from smoking, he may increase the tax on tobacco: to
increase trade he may decrease the tax on certain goods
(or make hire purchase easier) so that more people will
buy them.

Parliament debates the Budget very carefully because
it is so important, and when it has been passed (as it
usually is) the new changes are put into effect. If there
are unexpected changes in the economy — perhaps the
country suddenly needs large sums of money for an
emergency — there may be a supplementary budget in
the autumn. These are the budget figures for 1985:

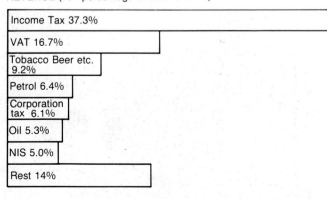

REVENUE (% = percentage of total revenue)

Income Tax 37.3%	
VAT 16.7%	
Tobacco Beer etc. 9.2%	
Petrol 6.4%	
Corporation tax 6.1%	
Oil 5.3%	
NIS 5.0%	
Rest 14%	

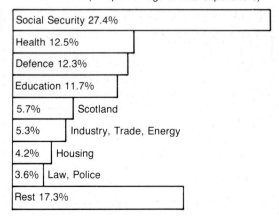

EXPENDITURE (% = percentage of total expenditure)

Social Security 27.4%	
Health 12.5%	
Defence 12.3%	
Education 11.7%	
5.7%	Scotland
5.3%	Industry, Trade, Energy
4.2%	Housing
3.6%	Law, Police
Rest 17.3%	

Taxation

The Government raises money by (1) direct taxation, (2) indirect taxation, and (3) borrowing.

Direct taxation. This is the money which has to be paid to the Government on demand. It is collected by the Inland Revenue department. The main direct taxes are: income tax; corporation tax (a kind of income tax on companies instead of on individuals); stamp duties (taxes paid when houses or stocks and shares are bought); capital gains tax (a tax on the profit made when valuable possessions or shares are sold); inheritance tax (a tax when large sums of money are given to a person or are passed on under wills); and petroleum tax (a tax which oil companies have to pay on each barrel they get from the ground. This is not the tax the motorist pays at the garage).

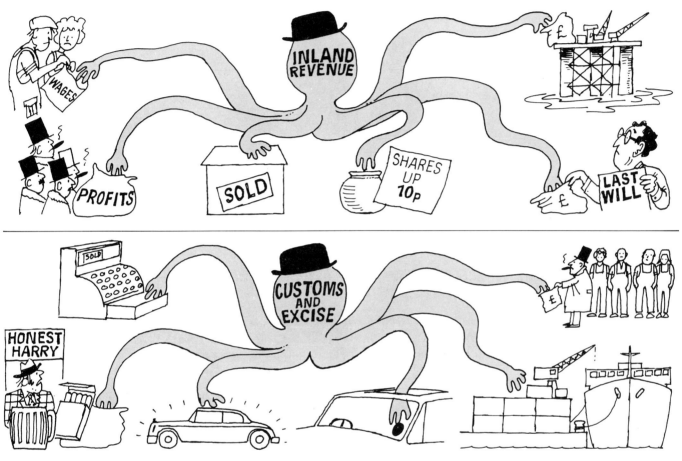

Indirect taxation. These are taxes which are added to the cost of goods and services which people buy. They are collected by the customs and excise department. The most important indirect taxes are Value Added Tax (an extra 15% of the cost of most goods is added and goes to the Government); special taxes on alcohol, tobacco, new cars and betting — these are in addition to VAT; EEC tax (a special customs duty on some goods coming from non-EEC countries); motor vehicle licences; and national insurance surcharge (a tax paid by businesses for each worker they employ).

Borrowing. The Government gets money from the public in the form of loans. These are mainly from Treasury (gilt-edge) and other bonds, and national savings.

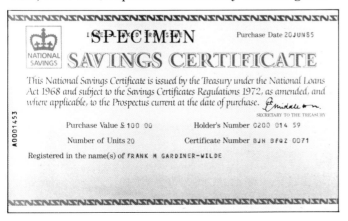

THE LEGAL SYSTEM

Laws are based on: (1) Legislation — acts of Parliament or local authority bye-laws. (2) Common law — these are ancient laws and traditions largely from early times which form the basis of the British legal system. They remain in force unless Parliament (or sometimes judges) change them. (3) Today some laws made by the EEC apply — maximum weight of lorries, certain food regulations etc.

Criminal law. Crimes are acts in which a person knowingly breaks a law passed by Parliament. Examples are: murder, robbery and dangerous driving.

Civil law. Disputes between individuals or groups of individuals about rights and duties to each other. Examples are: debts, divorce, wills, libel and property rights.

Criminal law

Juvenile courts. In law children under the age of 10 cannot commit a crime because they have not reached the age of criminal responsibility. In exceptional cases, however, such children may be put in homes because they are in need of care and attention. People between 10 and 17 charged with crimes are dealt with at juvenile courts. Charges are heard by magistrates in an informal atmosphere so that the young people are not too frightened. Punishments range from reprimands to being sent to certain institutions.

Magistrates' courts. All adult offenders must appear first at a magistrates court. The case is heard by two or more lay (ie not legally trained) magistrates, who are helped on points of law by the Clerk of the Court, who is a lawyer. There is no jury. The magistrates can impose fines of up to £2 000 or sentences of up to 6 months in prison. If they feel that these are not enough, they can send the convicted person to the Crown Court, which can impose any sentence. Less serious charges such as motoring offences or minor crimes are usually dealt with in magistrates courts.

Crown courts. More serious offences are dealt with at Crown Courts, which can impose any sentence up to life imprisonment. If the accused pleads 'not guilty' there must be a jury. Moderately severe cases are tried by a circuit judge or a recorder, who sometimes sit with magistrates. Very serious offences such as murder are tried by a high court judge alone. An accused person can conduct his or her own defence but rarely does so because the law is so complicated. If a lawyer is used it must be a barrister, and not a solicitor.

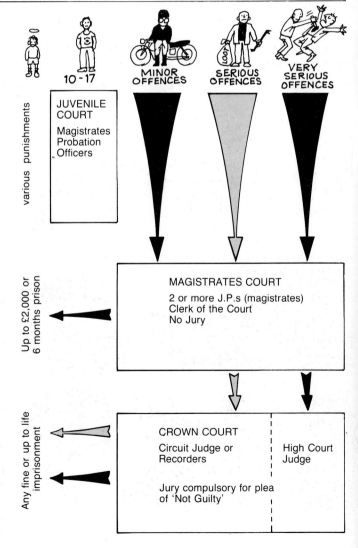

Civil law

Disputes between two people, or groups of people, can be settled in the civil courts.

Magistrates' courts. Magistrates sitting in private can settle minor disputes. These are mainly domestic quarrels, such as non-payment of maintenance to deserted or divorced wives, custody of children when the parents part, adoptions, etc.

County courts. More serious disputes are taken to the county court where they are heard by a judge — usually a circuit judge. They deal with disputes over contracts, hire purchase payments, rent acts, racial and sex discrimination, unfair dismissal, bankruptcies (outside London) and undefended divorces. Defended divorce cases must go to the High Court.

High Court of Justice. The more difficult cases, and ones which often involve large sums of money, are dealt with in the High Court of Justice. This is divided into three parts:
1. Chancery, which deals with wills and settling the estates of people who have died.
2. Queens Bench, which deals with commercial and shipping law.
3. Family, which deals with family matters such as divorces, wards of court, etc.

Civil courts do not punish people because no law has been broken but they decide which of the two people, the plaintiff and the defendant, are in the right and can enforce their decision by:

1. Damages. The court can order one person pay the other a sum of money which the judge (or sometimes a jury) think compensates them for what has been done, as for example, in libel or slander.

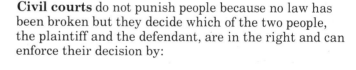

2. Seizure of property and attachment of wages. In cases of debt the court can order the defendant's property to be taken and sold to pay the money owing. In cases such as non-payment of maintenance, the court can order the money to be taken from the defaulting person's wages.

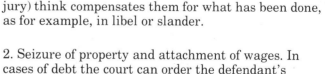

3. Injunctions. The court can order a person to stop doing certain actions which have been causing a nuisance to the other — repeatedly returning to the home of a divorced spouse, for example.

Contempt of court. All of these judgements of the civil court have the force of law, and disobeying becomes a criminal offence. This is called 'contempt of court' and the guilty person can be sent to prison until he or she agrees to carry them out.

DUTIES OF THE POLICE

Prevention of crime

Detection and arrest of criminals

Accidents

Protection of the public, property, and important people

Traffic duty

Assisting people in difficulty or with social problems

Guarding people in custody awaiting trial

Tracing missing people

Crowd control

The police in England and Wales are under the general authority of the Home Secretary and the Home Office. The Metropolitan (London) Police whose headquarters are New Scotland Yard, are controlled directly by the Home Office. In the rest of England and Wales there are regional police authorities working under the Home Office, each with its own force. When necessary the regional forces cooperate with each other. Some forces have specialised units such as mounted police, river police, traffic police, dog-handlers, CID and crime squads. In Scotland and Northern Ireland the police are under the control of the Secretaries of State for Scotland and Northern Ireland.

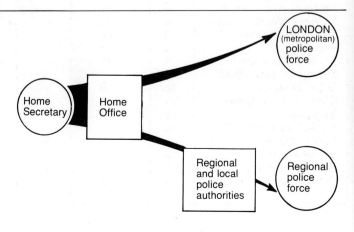

Questions

The nature of politics and central and local government

1. Political systems and parliament

Political Spectrum

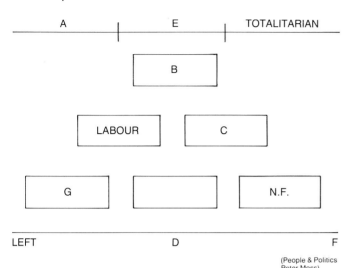

(People & Politics
Peter Moss)

(a) On your answer sheet, list the letters A to G and write next to them the words which should appear in the diagram above in their places.

(b) What do the words totalitarian and parliamentarian mean? Give an example of each of these terms.

(c) From your Social Studies work, describe what happens during a General Election Campaign and say how it is decided which party wins.

2. Political systems and parliament

Table of occupations of MPs elected June 1970

Occupations	Labour	Conservative	Liberal
Barristers	34	56	3
Solicitors	12	11	—
Journalists etc	25	35	—
Publishers	2	6	—
Public Relations	2	2	—
Teachers and lecturers	56	7	—
Civil service	3	2	—
Doctors	6	4	—
Farmers and landowners	3	40	—
Company directors	3	107	—
Accountants	2	5	—
Underwriters and brokers	1	22	—
Managers, executives	23	17	—
Other business	18	18	—
Clerical and technical	11	4	—
Engineers	19	3	—
Trade Union Officials	34	—	—
Party Officials	2	7	2
Mineworkers	20	—	1
Railway workers	5	—	—
Other manual workers	12	1	—

(a) From the information given in the table
  i) say which were the *3* most common occupations from which Labour MPs were drawn,
  ii) say which were the *two* most common occupations from which Conservative MPs were drawn.

3. Political systems and parliament

POLITICS

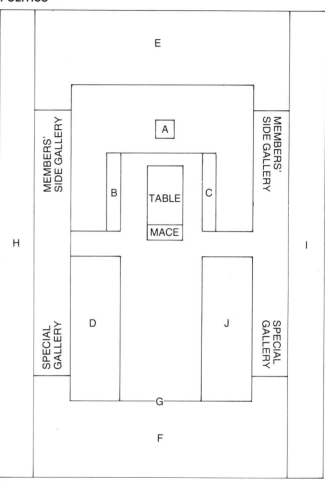

(a) Copy the following list onto your answer sheet, put next to them the letters (A-J) showing where they would appear on the plan above:

Public gallery   Mr Speaker
Government Back Benches   Government Front Bench
'Aye' Lobby   'No' Lobby
Press gallery   Opposition Front Bench
Other opposition parties   Bar of the house

(b) Which House of Parliament is shown in the plan above?

(c) Name *two* stages through which a Bill has to pass before it becomes an Act of Parliament.

(d) When a political party wins an election it forms the Government. State *two* main differences between Government and Parliament.

4. Political systems and parliament

Members elected at the general election of May 1979

PARTY	NO. OF SEATS
Conservative	339
Labour	268
Liberal/SDP Alliance	11
Scottish Nationalists	2
Plaid Cymru	2
Official Unionists	5
Democratic Unionists	3
Other	4
TOTAL M.P.'s	635

(a) How many more seats did the Conservative party have in 1979 than the Labour Party?

(b) Which of the parties shown in the above formed the government in 1979?

(c) What do the two nationalist parties named in the table hope to achieve?

(d) Some societies use a system of 'proportional representation' in elections. Explain how this works.

5. National government finance

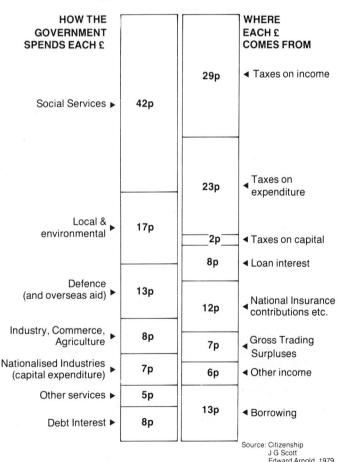

HOW THE GOVERNMENT SPENDS EACH £

- Social Services ► 42p
- Local & environmental ► 17p
- Defence (and overseas aid) ► 13p
- Industry, Commerce, Agriculture ► 8p
- Nationalised Industries (capital expenditure) ► 7p
- Other services ► 5p
- Debt Interest ► 8p

WHERE EACH £ COMES FROM

- 29p ◄ Taxes on income
- 23p ◄ Taxes on expenditure
- 2p ◄ Taxes on capital
- 8p ◄ Loan interest
- 12p ◄ National Insurance contributions etc.
- 7p ◄ Gross Trading Surpluses
- 6p ◄ Other income
- 13p ◄ Borrowing

Source: Citizenship
J G Scott
Edward Arnold. 1979

(a) What is the largest single item of government expenditure?

(b) Give two examples of "Taxes on expenditure".

(c) What is the difference between a direct tax and an indirect tax? Give examples.

(d) Discuss the social and economic consequences of lowering the expenditure on

    i) defence
    ii) nationalised industries
    iii) local and environmental services

6. The legal system

Write an essay on the Legal System, use the following as guide lines.

(a) The following persons are all to be found in the criminal courts of England and Wales. Give a brief description of the work done by:

    i) magistrates
    ii) barristers
    iii) juries
    iv) judges

(b) What are the chief differences between a magistrates' court and a crown court in relation to the composition of the court, the types of offence dealt with and the punishments given?

(c) What are the possible advantages and disadvantages of each of these courts for an accused person on trial?

7. The legal system

Look at the illustration of the courtroom and answer the following questions:-

(a) Identify the eleven people, indicated by the letters A-K, in the illustration, using the list below.
(N.B. there are 12 jobs listed, so 1 is not applicable to the illustration)

(i) Chairman of the Bench.
(ii) Clerk to the Justices.
(iii) Defence counsel.
(iv) Fellow magistrate.
(v) Journalist.
(vi) Member of the Public.
(vii) Police Officer in charge of the Court List.
(viii) Police officer on duty.
(ix) Prosecuting Counsel.
(x) Usher.
(xi) Witness.
(xii) Accused.

(b) What kind of court is shown in the illustration?

(c) Give four examples of the type of cases the court in the illustration would deal with.

(d) Name two other kinds of court.

(e) Give one example from each of these courts of the sort of case that these courts would deal with.

8. The duties of the police

(a) Are crimes more likely to be committed in urban or rural areas? Give reasons for your answer.

(b) What do you understand by the term 'community policing'?

(c) How is the Police force organised in London?

(d) Describe three ways, not linked with crime, in which the Police help the public.

PRISON AND PROBATION

A judge or magistrates sentencing a person found guilty has many options (see p.89). There are custodial sentences (prison, borstal, training or detention centres) or non-custodial sentences (reprimand, binding over, fines, suspended and deferred sentences, and probation).

Prison (custodial sentence)

Most of Britain's prisons are very old and not suited to today's numbers or conditions.

1. Prison seems to have little reforming effect on most prisoners — 94% of all men entering prison have been in at least once before.

2. People learn more about crime in prison that they ever could outside, and many emerge far more skilful criminals.

3. Prison is a waste of manpower and money: the prisoners contribute nothing to society, and cost an average £310 a week to keep.

4. Prison life and conditions are degrading, and do little to help people to fit into society again when released. Yet it seems essential to keep some form of prison for the protection of society against people who are violent or who are in some other way a threat to the community. Deprivation of liberty is the ultimate threat we have now that there is no death penalty.

Probation (non-custodial sentence)

Probation is an attempt to prevent a young (17+) first offender found guilty of serious crime, from continuing a criminal career. Instead of being given a custodial sentence they are put 'on probation' for anything from 6 months to 3 years. They continue to live a near-normal life at home and work under the supervision of a probation officer. If their home conditions are bad they may be required to live in a residential hostel, and in some cases they may have to attend special day-training centres to learn a trade.

The persons on probation have to pay regular visits (often weekly) to the probation officer and if their behaviour is not satisfactory they can be taken back to the original court for re-sentencing. This may now be custodial, an extension of the probation order, or any other form of punishment.

Probation officers are attached to the courts and are administered by a committee made up of local JPs and people who have legal or social welfare experience. The probation service also runs the community service scheme, after-care for prisoners released and often the residential hostels and day-training centres.

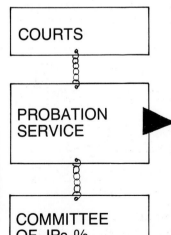

```
COURTS

PROBATION
SERVICE

COMMITTEE
OF JPs %
PEOPLE WITH
LEGAL & SOCIAL
WELFARE
EXPERIENCE
```

Supervision of offenders on probation.

After-care for ex-prisoners — accommodation, jobs, readjustment to freedom.

Running residential hostels, day training centres for those ordered to attend.

Running community service projects. People on probation can be ordered to do up to 240 hours painting old people's homes, building adventure playgrounds etc.

Alternatives to present punishments

It was only 300 years ago that 18 people were burned alive at St Osyth in Essex for being 'witches': it was only 21 years ago that the last person was executed by hanging in Britain for murder. Everyone now considers death at the stake a terrible barbarity, and most people think of execution by any means as uncivilised. Who can say whether the people of the next century may regard imprisonment as equally barbarous? These are some of the alternatives suggested.

Weekend prison. Convicted persons should keep up their normal life, living at home and following their normal work so that they maintain their families, but go to prison for each weekend until they have served their sentence. This is being done in Sweden, especially for serious motoring offences.

Compensation. Convicted persons should be made to work, under supervision if necessary, to repay the damage they have inflicted on an individual or on society. Courts can under certain circumstances order this at the moment, but it is rarely done and could perhaps be extended.

Deprivation of pleasures and facilities. The principle of taking away privileges from people who have done wrong but otherwise leaving them to a normal life is well established. For some motoring offences drivers have their licences taken away: some football hooligans are banned from attending matches for a period. Perhaps this principle could be extended.

Restitution to society. Some people suggest that criminals might make some restitution to society by being used as guinea pigs for medical work — testing new drugs and techniques for example. These would not be dangerous experiments — in the USA volunteer prisoners were given remission for taking part in male contraception pill tests.

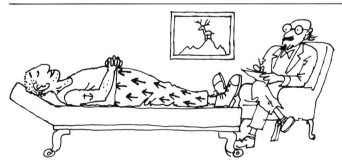

Medical/psychiatric treatment. This is of course practised today, but some people say that its scope should be extended as almost all criminals are mentally sick people. The violent, the psychopaths and sex offenders could be sedated with drugs which interfered as little as possible with their normal lives. Other less serious offenders could be treated by less extreme psychiatric methods.

Useful commercial work. Convicted criminals should be made to work on special projects or commodities which were useful and commercially valuable. The sale of their products could go towards the upkeep of the prisoners, or else be regarded as help for the country. This idea is fiercely opposed by trade unions as they say it would be unfair competition.

LOCAL GOVERNMENT

The national government is far too busy with general policy, foreign affairs, defence, money and overall control to involve itself in the detailed running of the country at a local level. This is left to local government which, apart from Northern Ireland, is based at the moment on a two-tier system. There is one council for each large or very densely populated area (say a county or a big city) which deals with the more important aspects affecting the whole area, and a number of smaller councils for more local affairs. In England and Wales there are county councils, which are divided into a number of district councils. In Scotland there are regions, subdivided into districts, but in Northern Ireland there are only district councils. London has the City and 32 borough councils. There is no overall authority apart from some important services such as education (Inner London Education Authority — ILEA), the Metropolitan Police, and the Fire Services.

In rural areas there are parish councils (community councils in Wales and Scotland) in most parishes. These have very little power but are useful for passing on the village opinion on local planning and similar matters to the district councils.

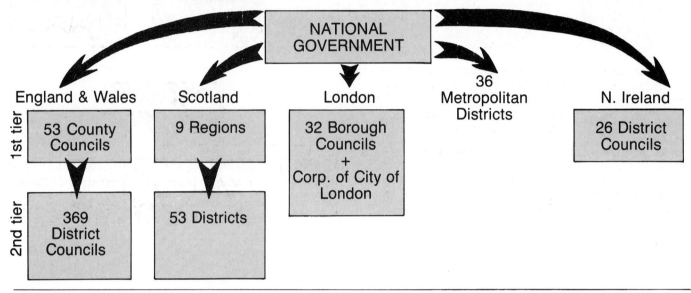

NATIONAL GOVERNMENT

	England & Wales	Scotland	London	36 Metropolitan Districts	N. Ireland
1st tier	53 County Councils	9 Regions	32 Borough Councils + Corp. of City of London		26 District Councils
2nd tier	369 District Councils	53 Districts			

Responsibilities of local government

County councils are responsible for the matters that affect the whole area they cover and which would be difficult to coordinate if done on a local (district) basis. District councils are responsible for matters which are best dealt with on a local basis.

Conservation   Consumer Protection

COUNTY COUNCILS

Police   Education   Major Planning   Roads and Traffic   Fire Brigades   Libraries   Solid Refuse Disposal   Social Services

DISTRICT COUNCILS

Local Planning   Building Regulations   Some Road Maintenance   Refuse Collection   Cemeteries and Crematoria   Environmental Health

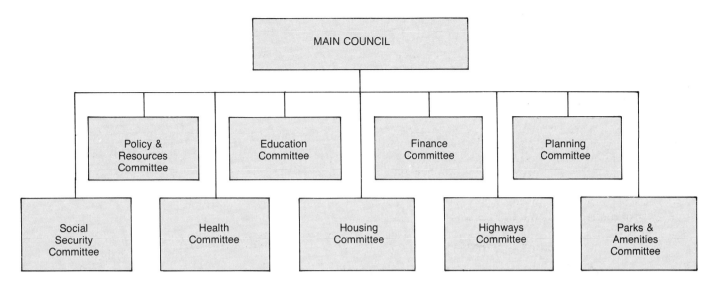

The chart above shows some of the many committees which make up the local government organisation. Some of these are more important than others — the four on the top row are very important, and the chairmen of these have considerable power.

Many of these committees are divided up into sub-committees to deal with particular aspects of their work. For example, some of the sub-committees into which the main education committee is divided are shown in the chart on the right.

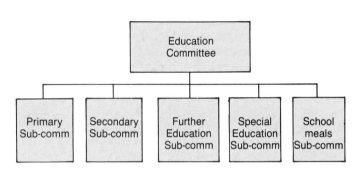

Administration

The decisions reached by the committees and sub-committees are approved — or rejected — by the main council meeting, and it is then left to the authority officials and other employees to carry them out. 3 million people in Britain are employed in local government — almost 1 in 10 of all workers. The chief administrative officers of the authority (who are usually appointed by the sub-committee with which they will have to work) and their staff work out the details and instruct the various employees what to do.

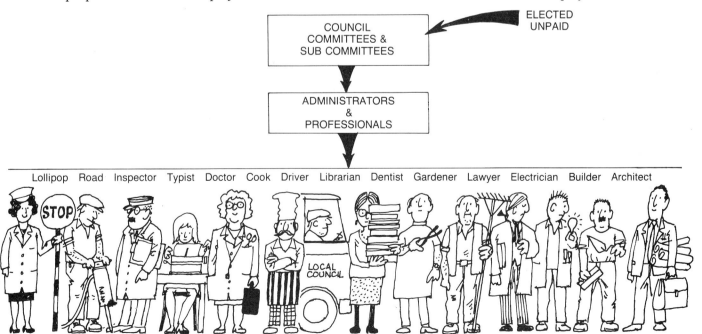

Council elections

All councillors are elected by the people of the area and hold office for four years at a time.

Electors
Any British, Irish or Commonwealth citizen over 18 may vote in local government elections if they are registered in that area by living or working there. In practice only about one third of the electors bother to vote at these elections.

Councillors
Councillors are elected for four years. County councils have 60 -100 members, district councils 30 - 80. Candidates can be anyone over 21 who is registered to vote in that area. Employees of a council are not allowed to become candidates for *their own* council, though they may for another. Councillors are not paid, but may claim expenses for travelling, food etc.

Chairman
The councillors elect a chairman from their number every year.

All county council seats are voted for every four years.

Elections for all seats on councils				Elections for all seats on councils	

1990   1991   1992   1993   1994

District councils may choose for all seats to be voted for every four years like the county councils, or else for one third of the seats every year, except the fourth when the county council elections take place.

No District Council Elections	⅓ Councillors retire — Elections for ⅓ of council	⅓ Council retire	⅓ Council retire	No District Council Elections	⅓ Councillors retire — these elected in 1991

1990   1991   1992   1993   1994

Party politics

For local government elections the county or town is divided up into areas on the basis of population. In towns these areas are called 'wards'. Most candidates are put up by the main political parties, but often these candidates will emphasise local issues rather than national ones: defence spending would not be a great vote-winner on a large housing estate, but a new secondary school for the pupils would. In local government elections however, there are many more independent candidates, or candidates representing local pressure groups or interests, such as Rate-payers' Party. The elections themselves are exactly the same as those for Parliament.

Local government finance

Local governments together spend about £33 000 000 000 a year — or about £600 for every person in the country. This expenditure is made up roughly as follows.

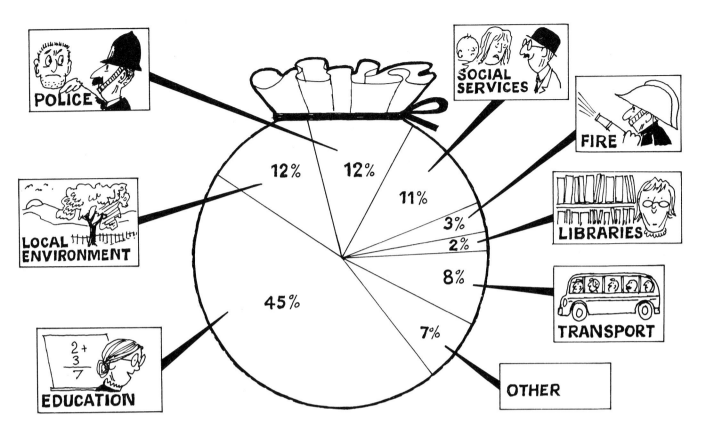

Local authorities get their income for the day-to-day running of their area from two main sources: Government; and the rates (see p.94). When they need money for some long-term capital project such as slum clearance, new housing, they may borrow from the public by means of loans, stocks or bonds. They have to pay interest on these, of course, and may not use this loan income for normal expenses such as education and other services without permission from the Government.

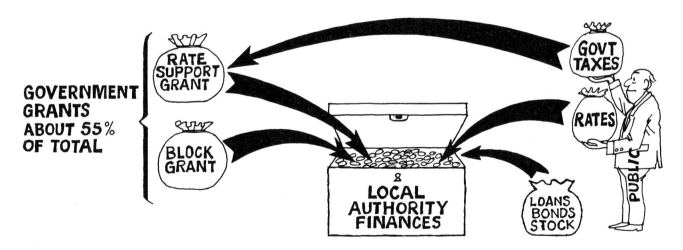

Government grants. There are two kinds of government grant: a block grant and a rate support grant. The *block grant* is a sum of money given to a local authority to help it meet its services to the public, so that standards are about the same all over the country. The *rate support grant* is a separate sum to help the authority keep its rates down to a reasonable level. The Government does, however, decide roughly what each council should spend, and limits its grant to its share of this amount. This means that councils cannot spend large sums of money on luxury schemes which would make them popular with voters at the next council election. It also means that councils in some deprived areas may not be able to afford some schemes which would improve the way of life for many citizens.

Rates

Rates are a local tax paid by occupiers of land or property to help pay local government expenses. The council's rating department fixes a *rateable value* for each property or piece of land (except farm and buildings and places of worship) in its area. Each year the council works out how much money it will need in addition to the central government grants, and then fixes an *amount in the pound* which has to be paid in rates.

If, for example, a house has a rateable value of £300 and the rates for that year were 150p in the pound, the occupier would pay

$$300 \times 150 = £450$$

The occupier also pays national taxes — VAT, income tax and so — part of which is used for government grants to local authorities.

Poll tax community charge

Many people think that rates are unfair and new ways of collecting money for local government services are being considered. One of these is the poll tax, or community charge.

Rates are a tax on *property*. A poll tax is a tax on *people*. 'Poll' is an old word meaning 'a head' so that in a poll tax every adult has to pay a certain amount to the local authority.

Rates v. Poll tax

Rates

Rates are unfair because they are based on where a person lives, and not the amount of services such as education, sewerage, street lighting and cleaning that the house uses.

Poll tax

Poll taxes are unfair because everyone, whatever their income, has to pay the same. The burden will fall more heavily on poorer families while the richer will often pay less.

Rates are easy and cheap to collect so that more of the money goes to provide services provides by the local authority.

Poll taxes are more complicated to collect. They need more staff so that less money goes to services.

Rates are fairer because the richer people generally live in larger houses and so pay more tax than the poorer, who have smaller homes.

Poll taxes are fairer because everyone has to pay. Of 35 million adults in England and Wales, only 18 million pay rates.

Organisation of local government

Each authority can decide its own form of internal organisation, but most of them operate a 'committee' system. The main council meeting in full decides policy and makes final decisions, but it can delegate all powers (except rates, loans and some other financial matters) to committees and sub-committees, all of which are made up of members of the main council. As the councillors are ordinary people with many different jobs, they cannot usually be expected to understand the technical details of some of the matters they have to decide upon. In such circumstances they are advised by professional officials employed by the local authority — the county surveyor would give advice to the planning committee, the county architect to the housing committee, the medical officer of health to the health committee, and so on.

Public participation

The public can take much more part in local government, because it seems to be of much more immediate importance to them than national government. The things the local government does usually affects them personally, and for most people in Britain it is much easier to go to the town hall to listen to a council meeting than to go to London to the Houses of Parliament.

The public can have much more influence on their councillors than it has on its MPs because they live locally. The people can bring pressure to bear on the councillors:

- Telephoning, writing to, or meeting councillors

- Writing letters to local papers

- Organising demonstrations or petitions

- Joining a pressure group

Questions

1. Punishment

1509-1547	Henry VIII's reign. Estimated 72,000 executions took place.
1714-1830	During this period, 156 new offences were made capital.
1819	Total of 220 different offences carried the death penalty.
1832	Capital punishment abolished for cattle, horse and sheep stealing.
1833	Capital punishment abolished for housebreaking.
1836	Capital punishment abolished for forgery.
1837	Capital offences reduced to 15.
1841	Capital punishment abolished for rape.
1861	Capital offences reduced to 14.
1868	Public executions abolished.
1908	Capital punishment abolished for persons under 16.
1922	Capital punishment abolished for infanticide.
1931	Capital punishment abolished for pregnant women.
1932	Capital punishment abolished for persons under 18.
1957	Capital offences reduced to 6.
1965	Capital punishment abolished altogether for 5 years.
1970	Total abolition of capital punishment confirmed by Parliament.

(a) In what year were the number of offences for which death was the penalty reduced to only 14?

(b) What happed in 1908 according to the chart above?

(c) What one point does the chart tell you about capital punishment?

(d) From your Social Studies work, say what you think about bringing back the death penalty for certain offences.

2. Prisons

The prison population
thousands of prisoners at end of June of each year

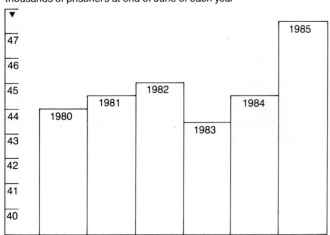

Read the information below and answer the following questions.

Many people believe that crime has increased in recent years. One piece of evidence used to strengthen this belief is the number of people in prison.

Many reasons have been suggested as to why some people break the law, it has been said that law-breaking is connected with some or all of the following:

- A having other criminals in the family
- B being unemployed
- C social class
- D poverty
- E a mother working outside the home
- F broken homes
- G truancy from school
- H success or failure in education.

(a) How many people were in prison at the end of June 1985?

(b) How has this number changed since 1980?

(c) What other evidence, apart from prison numbers, can people give to show that law breaking has increased?

(d) Choose *two* of the reasons listed above and explain how *each* may sometimes lead to criminal behaviour.

(e) "There is more and more crime in our society. The only way to deal with this is to put more criminals into prison for longer periods."

Do you agree or disagree? Give reasons for your answer.

3. Local government

Local Council Expenditure						
	1965		1970		1976	
Services	£m	% of total	£m	% of total	£m	% of total
Education	1,227	42.7	1,957	40.0	6,109	41.4
Police	190	6.6	341	6.7	1,024	7.0
Fire Service	47	1.6	72	1.5	243	1.7
Roads + lights	194	6.8	254	5.2	691	4.7
Sewerage + Refuse	138	4.8	162	3.3	331	2.2
Parks	52	1.8	74	1.5	275	1.9
Libraries, Museums	36	1.3	59	1.2	186	1.3

(a) On what service did the local councils spend 40.0% of their total budget in 1970?

(b) How much altogether did the local councils spend on parks in 1965 + 1970 + 1975?

(c) Which service do the local councils spend least on?

(d) From your Social Studies work, write all you can about *two* other services that local councils help to pay for.

Local Authorities' Pattern of Revenue and Expenditure 1982

Where each £ comes from (new pence)	REVENUE	EXPENDITURE	How each £ was spent (new pence)	
		10	Social Services	
		8	Police	
Local rates	36	2	Fire service	
		34	Education	
		3	Libraries, museums, parks, etc.	
Central government grants	47	5	Highways & planning	
		2	Refuse	
		9	Other services	
		13	Debt interest	
Miscellaneous fees, interests, rents, trading surpluses, etc.	17	3	Housing	
		11	Surplus	

TOTAL £33 834 million

4. Local government

(a) Look at the diagram, then answer the questions below.

   (i) What is meant by the term 'local authority'?

   (ii) What is the difference between revenue and expenditure?

   (iii) What is the largest source of revenue for local authorities?

   (iv) Out of each pound of expenditure, how much is spent by local authorities on social services and education?

   (v) A person earns £8,000 per year, owns her own house and spends £2 each week at an ice-skating rink run by the local authority. Show how she contributes to the revenue of her local authority in *three* different ways.

(b) A local authority decides to charge £1 for admission to its museum.

   (i) Give *two* reasons why people might support this decision.

   (ii) Give *two* reasons why people might oppose this decision.

(c) The rating system has been much criticised recently. Outline the arguments for and against the present system of local rates.

The development of ideas and attitudes

THE MEDIA

The chart below shows the main aspects of what we call *the media*. The *mass media* means the media which is seen, read or heard by the great majority of the population. The figures on the right hand side of the chart below show just how great the 'mass' is — the total population of Great Britain is about 55 million so that each person must have contact with several aspects of the media each day. This is why it is so powerful, so important — and can be so dangerous.

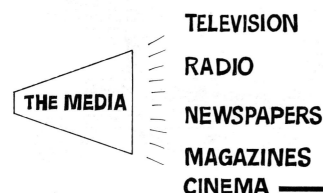

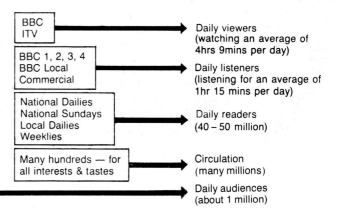

BBC / ITV	Daily viewers (watching an average of 4hrs 9mins per day)
BBC 1, 2, 3, 4 / BBC Local / Commercial	Daily listeners (listening for an average of 1hr 15 mins per day)
National Dailies / National Sundays / Local Dailies / Weeklies	Daily readers (40 – 50 million)
Many hundreds — for all interests & tastes	Circulation (many millions)
	Daily audiences (about 1 million)

THE MAIN PURPOSES OF THE MEDIA (IN ADDITION TO MAKING A PROFIT FOR THE OWNERS) ARE

TO INFORM

News, current affairs, sport, background to news.

TO ENTERTAIN

Drama, comedy, sport, quizzes, music, cartoons, childrens programmes etc.

TO EDUCATE

Documentaries, discussions, interviews, articles, specialist magazines, cooking, gardening and Open University programmes etc.

Importance of the media

The average person in Britain spends about 30% of waking time with some aspect of the media. This is almost as much as the time spent at work, so that the media must have a great influence on our lives.
The media comes from so many different sources, and is manipulated by so many different people that it can affect the way we look at almost anything in our world — politics, entertainment, the opposite sex, religion, other nations, the things we buy.

Television and radio

Television and radio broadcasting in Britain are run by two organisations, the BBC (British Broadcasting Corporation) and IBA (Independent Broadcasting Authority). Both of these were set up by the Government, though it has no control over them except that they must comply with the regulations laid down in the broadcasting acts. These include what may and may not be transmitted, and the maximum time allowed for advertisements on independent broadcasting.

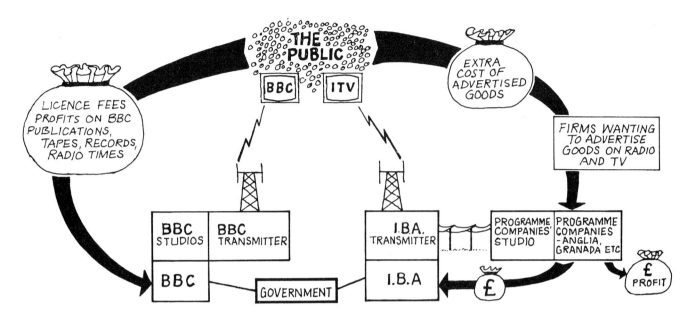

The British Broadcasting Corporation (BBC)

The BBC is headed by a committee of part-time governors appointed by the Queen (with her advisers) who make the broad policy decisions. The day-to-day running is done by full-time directors and their staff. The BBC has its own studios and outside broadcast units, makes its own programmes and broadcasts them from its own transmitters. It is a vast organisation employing many people — technicians, drivers, administrators, lawyers, doctors, artists, craftsmen and many others. The cost was £775 million in 1985, and all of this comes directly from the public (1) in TV licence fees, and (2) from the profits on BBC books, audio and video tapes, records and the Radio Times.

A small amount is made from the sale of BBC programmes to overseas countries.

The Independent Broadcasting Authority (The IBA).

The IBA is also headed by a board of part-time members, with full-time directors to do the actual running of the organisation. It has its own transmitters, but does not make any programmes. It sells the right to broadcast on its transmitters to independent programme companies — Granada, Anglia, London Weekend, Grampian, Ulster etc. These companies have studios and outside broadcast units and make the programmes we see on ITV. They pay for these, and make their (large) profits, by selling space on their programmes to firms who want to advertise. The firms naturally add the cost of the advertisement to the price of their product, so that the public does indirectly pay for ITV programmes.

Teletext

The BBC and IBA together have developed a teletext called Oracle by IBA and Ceefax by BBC. People who have a television set equipped with this system can call up hundreds of different 'pages' of printed information on the screen by pressing buttons. There are pages of the latest news, sports, motoring and weather details, prices of some goods, recipes etc. Subtitles of some programmes on the main television channels are available for the deaf.

The press

Britain is a nation of newspaper readers: the Government estimates that 77 out of every 100 people over 15 read or look at a daily paper every day. On Sundays the figure is higher still.

There are 11 national daily papers, excluding the very small-circulation Sporting Life and the communist Morning Star, and many local and regional daily, evening and weekly newspapers. The total daily sales of the eleven national dailies are about 15 million, but it is thought that on average each paper is read by two people. Evening newspapers sell about 7 million copies and Sunday papers about 18.

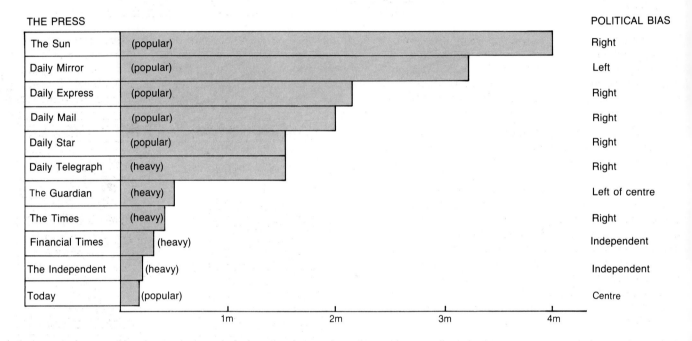

THE PRESS		POLITICAL BIAS
The Sun	(popular)	Right
Daily Mirror	(popular)	Left
Daily Express	(popular)	Right
Daily Mail	(popular)	Right
Daily Star	(popular)	Right
Daily Telegraph	(heavy)	Right
The Guardian	(heavy)	Left of centre
The Times	(heavy)	Right
Financial Times	(heavy)	Independent
The Independent	(heavy)	Independent
Today	(popular)	Centre

1m   2m   3m   4m

Popular and quality papers

The papers are divided into two groups: the 'heavy' or 'quality' newspapers; and the 'popular'. Readers of the 'heavies' tend to come from socio-economic groups A, B and C (see page 50). They expect in their papers long and detailed reports of political, economic, legal and foreign affairs, stock market information, results of minor sports such as rowing and fencing as well as the major ones, and serious articles on many subjects, as well as reviews of drama, music, books, films and TV. The popular papers are much easier to read than the heavies and include only a simple outline of the most important items of political, foreign and financial news. Their readers tend to prefer a 'human' angle to the news, with plenty of photographs. A large amount of space is given to the major sports, sensational crime, accidents and non-news items such as cartoons, horoscopes and light entertainment reviews.

This is how much space a 'popular' and a 'quality' paper gave to different subjects on a June day when there were no particularly important news items of any kind.

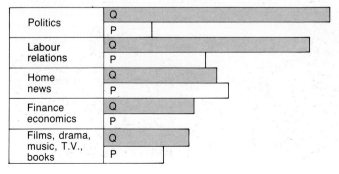

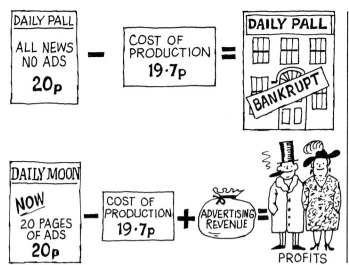

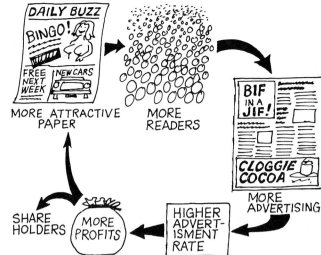

The price we pay for a newspaper only just covers the cost of production — wages, paper, distribution etc. Newspapers have to make a profit, and to do this they must sell space for advertisements. All firms want their advertisements to be seen by as many people as possible, and so they will normally put them in the papers which sell the most copies. Because of this demand these papers can charge more for their space and so make higher profits. The main object of most newspapers is therefore to increase their circulations.

Today the number of newspapers sold is fairly steady so that in general for one paper to increase its circulation another has to lose readers. The competition is very sharp because if sales fall below a certain level many advertisers stop using that paper and it has to close. In order to attract more customers newspapers may offer competitions with large prizes; extra supplements, often in colour; selected goods at 'bargain' prices; articles by, or about, famous people; more sensational news; more space to sport, cartoons, photographs of nudes; or trivial entertainment of all kinds. In the frantic search for higher circulations there is a great danger of standards falling and some newspapers becoming little more than adult comics.

As well as making profits newspapers often try to influence their reader's attitudes. This increases the newspapers' power, and can have an important effect on public opinion, especially on major national issues such as elections.

Selecting news. There is far more news than any paper can print. Some important items must be included, but the rest can be chosen, or left out, to suit the paper's ideas.

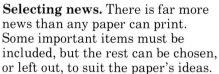

Editing. Almost every news item can be looked at in several ways, and newspapers can choose the way that suits them. Only parts of a speech or photograph for example may be used to give readers a good — or bad — impression.

Bias. Newspapers can write the articles with any political, social or other bias. While they probably would not deliberately tell lies, they can bend the truth in their own interests.

101

PROPAGANDA

Propaganda is the powerful and widespread effort by organisations, especially political, religious or social groups, to spread their ideas and practices. They do this by TV and radio programmes, speeches, rallies, posters and cinema depending on how much they can afford. The danger is that the organisation may be so convinced that it is right that it distorts the truth and leaves out any arguments against its own. This may slip into deliberate lies and falsifying evidence to prove the case.

In countries where there are several political parties, the opposition can put out its own propaganda to combat the government's. In one party states where the Government has total control over the media there is no alternative information, so that the people eventually believe what they are told. Dr Goebbels, Hitler's minister of propaganda, once said that if you tell people lies long enough they will believe them.

ПАПА, НЕ ПЕЙ

A Russian anti drinking poster (above) and a Chinese family planning hoarding (top right)

Two contrasting attitudes to the 1982 Falklands conflict

Daily Mail
TUESDAY, JUNE 15, 1982   17p

Chrissie
HER OWN STORY
—see Pages 24, 25

- Large numbers of Argentine soldiers threw down their weapons. They are flying white flags over Port Stanley •

—Mrs Thatcher in the Commons

VICTORY!

Maggie's

CENSORSHIP

Most people would agree that there are some things which should not be published or shown on the media, but there is disagreement about many others. What government papers should be available to the public, for example? What should and should not be permitted in the areas of violence, sex, religion and the ideas of extreme political and other organisations? Who should decide just what can be published?

In peace time in Britain there is officially no censorship of the media, but writers, editors, and producers cannot say just what they want. They have to be careful all the time that they do not make themselves liable for damages for libel, for prosecution under the Official Secrets Act or the Obscene Publications Act, or offend a large section of public opinion. This is in effect a kind of censorship.

Libel laws. If statements are published or broadcast which harm a person's reputation or character or cause loss of income, he or she can take action in the courts to get damages as compensation. The legal aspects of libel are very tricky, but damages can run into many thousands of pounds. There is also blasphemous libel for publishing material which mocks any aspect of the Christian religion.

Obscene Publications Acts. Anyone who writes or publishes material which the court decides is obscene is liable to be fined or even imprisoned. The difficulty with this act is that the court has to decide whether the material is obscene or not; people's ideas of obscenity differ widely. A few years ago certain swear words on the radio or tv, or nudity on the stage or cinema would have been considered obscene. Today they are common.

Official Secrets Act. Anyone who writes or publishes information which has been classified as secret is liable to be prosecuted. There are laws which can be used to prosecute people who give information on other illegal acts, such as undetectable ways to commit murder.

Offending public opinion. One of the strongest forms of 'censorship' is the fact that if the material upsets a very large section of the public they will not buy the paper or magazine, or watch that TV channel — for ITV channels this would means a disastrous loss of advertising revenue and jobs.

ADVERTISING

In western countries it is almost impossible to escape from advertising. It batters our eyes and ears — and sometimes even noses — all day long. The whole point of advertising is to get us to buy more, to buy new things, or to change from brand A to brand B so that merchants and manufacturers will make more profit. But though advertising may seem to be purely selfish, it does have some advantages for the public, even if by chance.

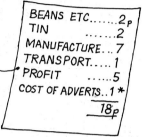

Advertising is expensive — a one minute spot on TV can cost £50 000. This cost is added to the price, so that the public pays more.

Advertising creates strong competition among traders, and can force down the prices of goods in the shops.

Advertising tempts us to buy more that we need — often goods which look good in the advertisement, but which have little real value.

Advertising encourages manufacturers to improve their goods to beat their rivals, so the public gets better products.

Advertising can bring out the worst in us by making us spend more than we can afford to do better than the neighbours.

Advertising increases the demand for goods. There is more work and wages for everyone — manufacturers, retailers, and many other people.

Advertising gives great scope for cheats to get our money by giving false ideas about the products they are selling.

Advertising lets us know just what is available, whether new products or improved models. We can compare prices and details before we go out to buy.

Advertisers are clever people. To get us to buy their goods they often play on the deepest human feelings. These are some of those emotions which can help advertisers to get money from our pockets into theirs.

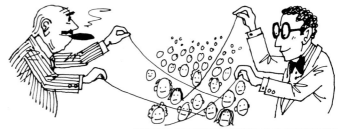

Fear. They can make us feel uneasy about our health, our appearance, the safety of our homes and other possessions, and the provision for our families if we died.

Greed. They try to make us believe we are getting great bargains, or are offering us the chance of getting something for nothing.

Pride. They appeal to our sense of wanting to be better-looking, better-shaped, smarter in appearance or have more expensive possessions than the average person.

Pleasure. They appeal to the pleasure instinct — the desire to enjoy ourselves.

Sense of laziness and luxury. They tell us that their product will make life much easier for us, give us greater comfort or a feeling of being superior.

Novelty and change. They appeal to people's desire to have the latest fashion, style or model and to have products with new ingredients, formulae etc.

Consumer protection in advertising

It is very easy for people to be deceived by advertisements, especially for mail order when they do not see the goods beforehand. Advertisements like the one below, which are obviously frauds, were common not many years ago, but today there are many regulations to protect the public from unscrupulous traders. Protection is given by the Government in the shape of laws, and codes of practice by the media and some manufacturers.

GOVERNMENT   MEDIA   MANUFACTURERS   THE PUBLIC

Government action. Many acts have been passed which make advertisements which are obviously fraudulent illegal. The people who issue such advertisements can be fined or even sent to prison. The Trades Description Act 1968 tightened up the rules not only on deliberately lying advertisements but also on those which are misleading. The act says that goods or services must conform exactly to the description in the advertisement. They must do, or be, just what was claimed for them. If they fail to do this the buyer can demand a return of the money — sometimes with compensation — and in serious cases the advertiser can be prosecuted by the Trading Standards or Consumer Protection departments of the local authority.

Codes of practice. The IBA and many newspapers and magazines have their own codes of advertising practice, and will not accept certain types of advertisement, or advertisements from firms whose honesty is doubtful. ITV, for example, will not take advertisements from political or religious organisations, or from fortune tellers and undertakers. It also bans advertisements for smoking 'cures' and some medical preparations. Cigarette advertising on TV is prohibited by law.

Some manufacturers have agreed among themselves not to use certain methods of advertising such as claiming that their product is better than that of another named rival — e.g. 'Hoover vacuum cleaners are far more efficient than Electrolux or Goblin'.

POLLS AND SURVEYS

Polls and surveys are a way of trying to find out what the majority of the population think by questioning a small sample. Advertisers, political parties and other organisations often need to find out (1) what people think of a particular product or idea, and why, (2) what changes they would like to see in it.
To get this information they often employ a poll company such as NOP, MORI or Gallup.

The poll company generally sends researchers into the streets to ask people questions, but they may also make enquiries over the phone, send questionaires through the post, or sometimes with previous arrangement, make in-depth interviews in people's homes. People are sometimes approached at random, but this may give an unrepresentative result — a poll taken mid-afternoon of a weekday would give a disproportionate number of retired people, women with small children and unemployed. Working men and women would not be adequately represented.

More often a 'quota' poll is used: people selected for interviewing are chosen as far as possible to be representative of the population as a whole, so that in every ten subjects questioned there should be about the numbers shown opposite. In addition there should be the correct proportion of people from ethnic minority groups, and people from different regions of the country.

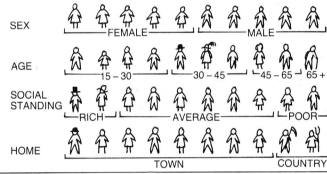

If a thousand or more people are interviewed a pattern begins to take shape, but it is not necessarily completely accurate. If people are fairly equally divided on the subject being investigated a poll can expect about 43% replies to be *YES*, and about 43% *NO*. This leaves about 14% of don't knows, liars, jokers and people who may change their minds. These people form the margin of error, and the result is doubtful.

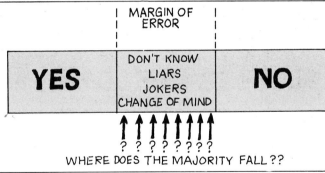

Commercial firms use opinion polls to find out where is the best place to sell their goods, at which group of people to aim their advertising, and how to improve the packaging, appearance or content of their product. Political and other organisations use polls to find out how the public feel about their policies, or about a specific issue, and they may adjust their ideas as a result of the findings. Polls are used widely before elections to try to estimate how people are going to vote — this may well influence the way the party or the candidate runs the campaign. Publication of poll forecasts may also affect the way people vote.

PRESSURE GROUPS

Pressure groups are organisations which try to influence authorities of all kinds to take, or to stop taking, a certain course of action. They are usually concerned only with one area of activity (unlike political parties) and may work at international, national or local levels. There are pressure groups with political goals (peace movements, trade unions and The City); environmental aims (Greenpeace, Friends of the Earth etc); religious (Lord's Day Observance Society), and many others. At local levels they may be concerned with such issues as new roads; demolition of old buildings; closing of schools, railway stations and bus routes; enclosing open spaces etc.

Some of the pressure groups are more or less permanent (peace movements, environmental organisations etc) while some are only temporary while that particular issue is in question (new motorways, closing of some local amenity etc) and disappear when they have achieved — or failed to achieve — their aim.

Pressure groups try to achieve their goals by:

Rallies, demonstrations and marches.

Media publicity — posters, leaflets, and general press coverage.

Direct action and taking legal action to stop the activity in the courts.

Lobbying MPs and councillors.

Publicity stunts.

Questions

The development of ideas and attitudes

1. Media

Read the following passage and answer the questions below.

Mass media as a form of communication are only about one hundred years old, and the greatest growth has come about in the last fifty. New technology may now be about to bring even greater changes in the ways by which information can be passed to large numbers of people.

As well as bringing benefits to many, the growth of mass communications has also brought problems. It raises questions about power and control in our society. Information and ideas can be contracted and influenced by rich individuals and small groups who own the mass media. Ordinary people could be made slaves to the interests and desires of such small groups.

(a) What is meant by 'mass media'?

(b) What makes communication by the mass media different from ordinary, face-to-face communications?

(c) What advantages have the mass media brought to ordinary people?

(d) How have industry and business benefited from the development of the mass media?

(e) Give examples of censorship which affect the media?

(f) "Many people feel that the media are too powerful in our life today." Do you agree or disagree? Give reasons for your answer.

2. Media

Write an essay on Mass Media, you should use the following as a plan.

(a) What is meant by the term "mass media"? Give *two* examples.

(b) Taking *one* example of the mass media which you have mentioned, describe some of the ways in which it is of benefit to people living in our society.

(c) It is often said that the mass media in this country should be more strictly controlled.

   i) What sort of controls over the media already exist?

   ii) Why do some people think that there should be further controls?

3. Media

Choose either an account of a violent football match or a fire in an old peoples' home and write two accounts of the item from the viewpoint of a quality newspaper and one as it would be in a popular newspaper. (Each account approx ½ page long).

4. Advertising

Read the following passage and answer the questions below.

Visitors to the USSR or Eastern European countries often say one of the first things they notice is there are few advertisements or efforts to persuade people to buy particular goods. This may be because the manufacture and sale of goods is organised differently in these countries and producers of goods do not need to make a profit.

The Russians and East Europeans would probably say that advertising only exists in the West to confuse people and to try to get citizens to 'want' things which they don't really 'need'. Prices in the West are increased by customers having to pay many hundreds of millions of pounds each year to cover the cost of advertising. However, Western manufacturers and the firms which produce advertisements would say this argument is unfair. They say that advertising gives valuable information about the products.

(a) According to the extract, what are two objections held by the Russians and East Europeans to advertising?

(b) What does the extract say is good about some advertising?

(c) Manufacturers in the West argue that advertising does not increase the cost of their products to the customer. How do they justify this?

(d) By using examples, say how you think that some advertising only confuses people and encourages them to spend their money foolishly.

(e) How can we protect ourselves from 'unfair advertising'?

(f) 'Advertisers want you to buy their products. Therefore you cannot trust what they say'. Do you agree? Give reasons for your answer.

5. Advertising

Total advertising expenditure by media.

Media	£m			% of Total		
	1960	68	76	1960	68	76
National newspapers	64	99	197	19.8	19.7	16.6
Regional newspapers	77	121	328	23.8	24.1	27.6
Magazines & Periodicals	40	50	92	12.4	9.9	7.7
Trade & Technical	31	46	103	9.6	9.1	8.7
Directories	2	8	31	0.6	1.6	2.6
Press Production Costs	15	23	58	4.6	4.6	4.9
Television	72	129	307	22.3	25.6	25.8
Poster & Transport	16	20	43	5.0	4.0	3.6
Cinema	5	6	8	1.5	1.2	0.7
Radio	1	1	21	0.3	0.2	1.8
Total	323	503	1188	100	100	100

(a) In 1968 in what form of media was £99 million spent?

(b) Directories accounted for what percentage of total monies spent for 1976?

(c) Which form of the media do advertisers spend less on than anything else?

(d) From your Social Studies work, say what effect you think advertising has on what we buy.

109

Power and authority

POWER

Power is strength.
Authority is the right to use that power.

Power can take many forms — physical; economic; moral/social/religious, or political.

Physical power. This is obvious: 'I am stronger than you, therefore I am going to threaten or hit you until you do what I want.' The physical power need not of course be entirely human strength: the thug with the club, the knife or the gun is using physical power, just as much as the nation that invades another with superior armed forces.

Political power is exercised not only by governments making laws to suit their own political theories, but also by voters and pressure groups.

Voters use their political power by voting out of office a particular party whose policies they do not like, or whose ideas have not worked. This kind of political power applies at national and local government levels, and also to smaller organisations such as the committee of the local football or social club.

Pressure groups can use the power of rallies, processions, protest meetings, petitions and other activities to try to make people in authority — national governments or local committees — change their policies or decisions.

Social/moral/religious power. At its simplest this is family pressure — 'You should not do that — your father/mother would not like it.' At its most powerful it is perhaps the pronouncements of great religious leaders on human behaviour and such issues as birth control. Social and moral pressures come from fellow pupils and students, from teachers, from the community all round us — '*We* do not do that...' '*All* of us are going to boycott lessons tommorrow...'

Economic power. This can be used at many levels. Parents refusing pocket money or support in further education unless their children do as they wish is a simple form of economic power.

Consumers can use economic power by refusing to buy certain goods, because they are too expensive or because they are made in places or conditions of which people disapprove — battery farming for example.

Big businesses can use economic power by selling goods at very low prices to force rivals into bankruptcy. Or they may buy up competing firms so that they can have a monopoly. Very large companies, especially multinationals, can even put great pressure on some governments by threatening to take their factories elsewhere.

Trade unions can use economic power to force employers to give higher wages or better conditions by paying members on strike.

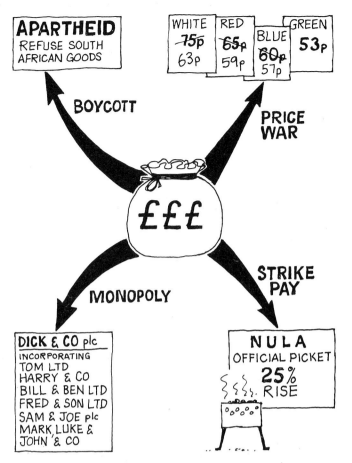

AUTHORITY

Authority is the *right* to use power. This permission comes from the law, or from custom and tradition. The highest authority in any country is the national government which makes the laws and authorises the police and the courts to enforce them. In democratic countries this authority is supposed eventually to come from the people themselves because they vote into power the Government which makes the laws.

At a lower level, the city or town or county council has authority to make local regulations, such as how the schools shall be run or the time the park shall be closed. This authority again comes in the end from the people who vote for the local councillors. Teachers, traffic wardens and many others have authority delegated to them by the local government.

In business, managers have the authority to organise the shop or office given to them by the owners or board of directors: in sport, the umpires and referees have the authority of the rule book, which has been compiled by the body governing that sport. At home, parents have the authority of tradition.

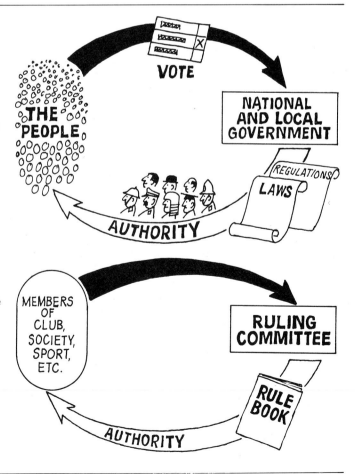

Pollution and conservation

POLLUTION

Pollution is a relatively modern problem. Hundreds of years ago in the small scattered villages people used mainly organic materials which decayed naturally; any industry — metal working for example — was on such a small scale it presented no problems. So few people lived in any one place that sewage and waste difficulties were negligible.

When more people began to live in towns and cities, and industries began to grow, there was an increasing pollution problem especially from sewage and waste. But this was still very minor. The arrival of the industrial revolution in the early nineteenth century, with its factories, steam engines, industries, chemicals, and its overcrowded cities at once made pollution a serious problem, though little was done at the time because of the greed and power of many factory owners. Though some of these earlier pollutions such as smoke, sewage and overcrowding — have decreased in the twentieth century, technology has brought new ones. These include far more dangerous chemicals, motor car fumes, oil and radiation.

As well as substances which cause physical harm, disagreeable sights and noises can make life more unpleasant, or even create mental diseases. These must also be considered as pollution. Below are some of the more usual pollutions encountered today.

Smoke. Smoke contains particles which damage the lungs, and make the environment filthy. More dangerous are chemicals such as sulphur dioxide, which combine with water in the air to form a strong acid. This eats into the stone of buildings, causing them to crumble. In the form of 'acid rain' it is destroying huge areas of forest in Europe.

Exhaust fumes. Motor vehicle exhaust fumes contain sulphur dioxide, as well as carbon monoxide which destroys blood cells, and substances which are thought to cause cancer. Lead (which is put in the petrol to make it more efficient) comes out into the atmosphere and is believed to cause severe mental retardation and stunted growth in young children who breathe it in large quantities.

Sewage and waste. Untreated sewage and liquids oozing from waste tips can soak into rivers and water supplies. Apart from being very unpleasant they can carry deadly germs such as typhoid and cholera.

Oil. Oil discharged or leaking from ships, while not normally dangerous to human life, is deadly to sea birds and fish. When it reaches the coast it can make beaches completely unusable.

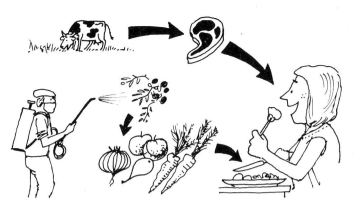

Agricultural sprays. Some highly poisonous chemicals are sprayed on crops to kill weeds, pests and plant diseases. Sometimes the spray is blown by the wind and breathed in by people, but more often it finds its way into fruit and vegetables, or into the animals that eat the grass, and so into human bodies.

Artificial fertilisers. These are put on crops to increase the yield and profits. Much of the chemical dissolves in rainwater, and eventually soaks back to the rivers and lakes. Here it may upset the balance killing fish and plant life, and making the water dead and filthy.

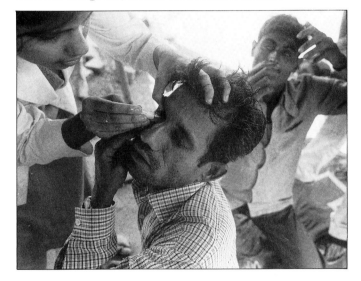

Industrial waste and leaks. Dangerous substances can be discharged (or leak) from factories into the air or water. In 1976, a chemical called dioxin leaked from a plant in Italy leading to severe injuries and deformities among local people. The area was uninhabitable for six years. In 1984 at Bhopal in India 2 000 people died and 180 000 were treated in hospital when poison gas leaked from a chemical plant.

Radiation. Radio-active substances used in nuclear plants and industrial equipment can cause severe forms of cancer, such as leukaemia, if there is leakage as a result of an accident. The accident at Chernobyl in the USSR in 1986 was an example.

Aerosols. The propellant gas in aerosols, while not immediately dangerous, is said to be accumulating in the upper atmosphere, where in the future it may cause disastrous effects to the whole world by increasing the temperature of the earth (glasshouse effect).

Visual pollution. These are things which make life less pleasant by spoiling the view. They include electricity pylons and industrial hoardings in beauty spots.

Aural pollution. Life can also be spoiled by unpleasant noises from factories; transport, especially aircraft; radios played loudly out of doors; public address systems; and noises transmitted through walls of badly-designed flats and houses.

CONTROLLING POLLUTION

Everyone agrees that pollution is bad, but getting rid of it is not as simple as it seems. If we stopped pollution most things would be more expensive, and some would not be available at all. Society has to decide just what it wants in goods and services, what it is prepared to pay for them, and how much pollution it is prepared to put up with.

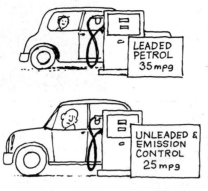

Some chemicals can be purified but the equipment is expensive so that the cost of electricity and manufactured goods would rise. Exhaust fumes can be made much cleaner by using unleaded petrol and expensive exhaust equipment.

Unleaded petrol is less efficient so that all transport costs would soar. Oil and other chemicals have become part of our way of life and we think we cannot manage without them. We can never eliminate the risk of some accidents.

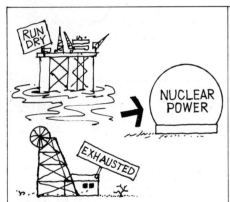

Coal and oil, the worst causes of pollution, are bound to run out. Unless some dramatic breakthrough is made in solar, wind or water power, the twenty-first century will have to use nuclear power. We should be experimenting with it now. If farmers abolished sprays and fertilisers, yields would fall sharply and prices of all foods increase. There would probably be lower quality foodstuffs. We must not forget too that one person's pollution may be another's pleasure.

Government action

In the last thirty years governments have been increasingly aware of the problems of pollution. Apart from being unpleasant, it is extremely expensive because it causes many illnesses and results in much lost working time. People too have rising living standards and will not tolerate conditions that existed in the past. The media and pressure groups have brought pollution and its dangers to the public notice, and science has found ways of dealing with it. All of these have forced governments to consider pollution very seriously.

Controlling pollution is, however, largely the responsibility of local authorities who have been given powers, and duties, by the national government in a number of acts. The most important ones are:

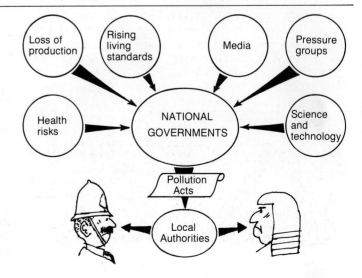

Clean Air Acts, 1956 and 1968. After a terrible 'smog' (a mixture of fog and smoke) in London in 1954 which killed 750 people a day, the Government decided that something drastic should be done. The Clean Air Act allowed local authorities to create some Control Areas in which smoke from chimneys was illegal. Today ⅔ of all town and cities are smoke free, and the effect has been dramatic. In central London there is now 40% more winter sunshine than 30 years ago. Local authorities have to approve the height of factory chimneys, and can enforce the installation of dirt and grit catchers in them. The emission of exhaust fumes from motor vehicles is also controlled.

Control of Pollution Act. 1974. This sets out the powers and duties of local authorities over pollution by waste, sewage, air and water. The authority must make sure it has adequate facilities for waste disposal and sewage, and can control what is allowed to run into rivers, lakes and the sea. It makes litter dropping a criminal offence with fines of up to £100.
Authorities can also make certain areas Noise Abatement Areas where noise from industrial and other premises can be controlled.
To show how effective these regulations can be, the River Thames has only ¼ of the pollution it had 30 years ago. Over 100 species of fish, including salmon, have been caught in the river which had become almost dead.

Prevention of Oil Pollution Act. 1971. This makes it illegal for any ship to discharge oil into the sea in British waters, and for a British ship to discharge oil anywhere in the world. There are also international agreements on this form of pollution.

Motor Vehicle Regulations. 1978. This sets out the maximum noise each type of vehicle is allowed to make. To make more noise, as measured on a special meter, is an offence. The International Civil Aviation Organisation has similar regulations about aircraft noise.

Radio-active Substances Act, 1960 (and later Acts 1965 and 1970). This Act controls the amount of radio-activity from equipment and especially radio-active waste. This has to be kept well below the amount which comes naturally from the earth and space.

Public Nuisance Acts. The police and local authorities have wide powers under Public Nuisance Acts to deal with — among other things — pollution which is not covered by other laws. This includes such things as noisy animals; offensive smells from private and industrial premises, smoke from garden fires. To prevent unsightly buildings or hoardings, people have to get planning permission from the local authority before they can be erected.

CONSERVATION

Anti-pollution tries to get rid of what we do *not* want in the environment: conservation tries to preserve what we *do* want, and to save for future generations some of the things we enjoy and use. Conservation is aimed at three main areas:

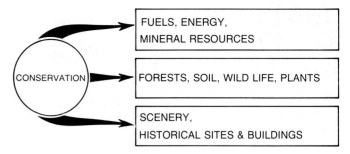

Fuels, mineral resources, energy. There are limited amounts of coal, oil, and minerals on earth, and when they have gone there is no way of replacing them. Today the world burns about 4 billion tonnes of oil and the same amount of coal each year, and some scientists believe that supplies will be exhausted within the next century. Some metals, such as copper, from known sources are already beginning to dry up, and it may soon be the same with iron, aluminium, and other minerals. As fossil fuels are our main source of energy many people think that we should be doing something to save them because they are also the chief source of many chemicals and drugs, and too valuable to waste by being burned.

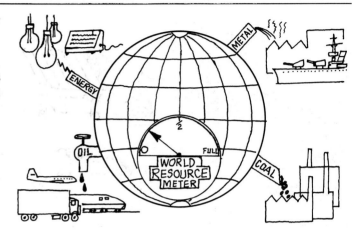

Forests, soils, animals and plants. Every year the world uses up a forest the size of England (about 13 million hectares) for paper alone — much faster than trees can be replaced. Thousands of hectares of land are being turned into desert or dust-bowls every year by bad farming — over-cropping, over-grazing and cutting down trees so that erosion takes place. Many species of animals and plants have become extinct because man has destroyed their environment by increasing farmland, draining marshes or using chemicals to increase crops. It is estimated that one species of plant or animal becomes extinct every day. The world needs more food for its increasing population and its rising living standards but this means more land for crops and less for the animals and wild plants.

Scenery, and historical sites and buildings. People in the future, who will have more leisure time than we have, will want the beautiful scenery and natural countryside that we enjoy. They will want to see the historical buildings and sites which are part of our — and their — heritage. With their improved technology they will probably be able to learn more about the past, than we can. Towns and cities and roads and industry gobble up land: in the interest of profit many old buildings, especially in towns where land prices are high, are demolished to make way for new office blocks and high-rise developments. Much of the beauty and interest of our world today should be preserved for generations to come.

THE NATIONAL TRUST

WWF

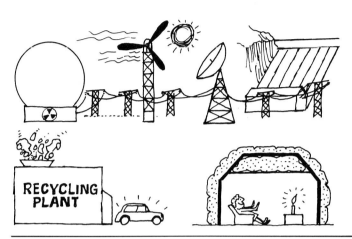

We should use more efficient transport which uses less petrol. Or we should use electric vehicles, as electricity can be generated without burning fossil fuels. We should have more efficient heating systems and make more use of the sun. Better insulation of buildings would prevent heat losses and save energy. Much more use should be made of other sources of power, such as water, wind, the sun and plants. Metals and other minerals should be replaced as far as possible by materials which can be manufactured from easily-available substances. Much of the metal, paper, glass and other things we waste today could be recycled so that future generations will have enough.

Many people feel that alternative forms of communication such as electronics, could save much paper, and so reduce the destruction of the forests. This would also help with the wildlife problem. Better education in agriculture, and strict government control to stop greedy farmers exhausting their land for profit could do much to prevent damage to the soil. Restricting the use of some chemicals in farming could help to preserve wild life, but large areas should be left untouched so that they have their natural habitats. Breeding rare animals in zoos can only be a temporary and unsatisfactory measure. Many governments and private organisations are taking steps by banning the most dangerous chemicals and setting up nature reserves.

Many national governments and local authorities, as well as private organisations and individuals are trying to save the heritages of their countries. Governments designate large areas of great beauty or interest as national parks where no development may take place: green belts (see page xx) are laid down round some towns and cities; preservation orders are placed on many old buildings of historical interest so that they cannot be demolished; there are fines for destroying sites such as prehistoric earthworks. Voluntary organisations undertake such works as restoring old barns and windmills, and cleaning out derelict canals. Private societies for preserving industrial steam railways and steam ships are found all over the country.

The world of work

WORK

What exactly is 'work'?

Must work involve doing something with the hands, or are people who just have to think working? Must work involve payment, or are you working when you are doing the job for pleasure or out of duty?

Who are the 'working classes'? Does it depend on the time put in — a doctor or lawyer may well work ten or twelve hours a day: a factory employee no more than eight. On the type of work? On the amount of money received? Does a person who has a large private income and who need not work, but does so, belong to the working class? Which of the following do you think are working class? Give reasons for those you think are not.

Specialisation

In the very earliest times each person or family made everything they needed: clothes, weapons, pottery, huts and equipment. Soon it was obvious that some people could make some things better than others, so *specialisation* or *division of labour* began. The good spear-maker would do little except make spears and barter them for food and clothing. Money was invented to make exchange of goods easier. Later on people learned how to get nature to help them in their work: animals for carrying and pulling; wind to drive boats; water to turn water mills. This was the beginning of technology, and the need for machines. Machines needed new kinds of skills, both to invent, make and operate, so that new specialised craftsmen appeared. Later still natural sources of power were replaced by steam, and later still by electricity. Today technology has become even more complicated by the introduction of electronics, which are really machines to watch other machines.

At each step in technology fewer people or a shorter time was needed to produce a certain article. With crude hand tools it might take ten people a week to make an iron pot; today with sophisticated machinery hundreds could be made in an hour. This has meant an increasing problem of what to do with the workers who are no longer required.

Technology and its effects

Making goods by hand was generally slow and resulted in variable quality. Most goods were expensive so few people could have them. This meant a low standard of living for the majority of people except the rich. Work was often done inefficiently with a great deal of wasted time, and there was little variety of products.

On the other hand, manual production did mean that there was work for most people.

Machine production is quick, cheap and of uniform quality. Far more people can have the goods so there is a higher standard of living. There are also many new kinds of goods (cars, radio, TV etc), as well as a much wider variety of existing ones. But, as few people can produce all of the vast numbers needed, there are often more unemployed. This is particularly serious today when electronic equipment allows machines to work by themselves, or with one person in charge of a large number of machines.

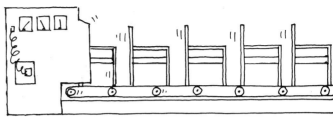

Seventy-five years ago no ordinary person's home would have had any of the things below — some because technology had not invented them, or because the limited production meant they were far too expensive for anyone except the very rich. On the other hand, only 5 people in every 100 of working age were unemployed, compared with 13 in 1986.

The chart below shows some of the effects of technology in the last 75 years. It shows how long it would take a man on the average industrial wage in 1910 and 1985 to earn enough money to buy the goods shown.

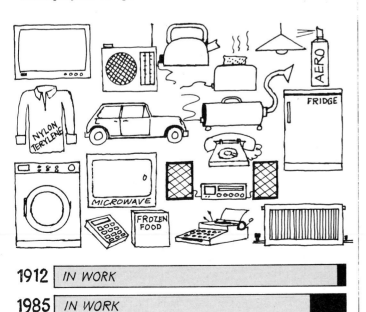

| 1912 | IN WORK |
| 1985 | IN WORK |

	1912	1985
Car	4 YEARS	6-8 MONTHS
Scotch	5½ HOURS	2 HOURS
Bicycle	3½ WEEKS	3 DAYS
Coat	5½ HOURS	2½ HOURS

Why work?

Most people dream of winning a great fortune and giving up work for ever. The chances of doing so are so remote that they can be ignored, and even if one did become independent, life without work would probably soon become boring to most people. While the majority would say that they work for the money, so that they can enjoy leisure, in reality there are other reasons quite as important.

CURRENT RATE PER WEEK				
TEACHER	DUSTMAN	DOCTOR	WAITRESS	ARCHITECT
~~£200~~	~~£100~~	~~£300~~	~~£75~~	~~£400~~
~~£170~~	~~£140~~	~~£310~~	£80	~~£200~~
£130	£150	£290	£88	£150
M.P.	POP SINGER	FARM WORKER	ARTIST	FACTORY WORKER
£300	~~£10,000~~	~~£90~~	~~£10~~	~~£140~~
£	£250	~~£150~~	~~£100~~	~~£150~~
		£250	£	£180

NATIONAL WAGES ASSESSMENT BOARD

Money. Obviously the first reason is to earn money, but there are strange differences in the way people are paid for work. The road sweeper and the barrister may work the same hours, and just as hard as each other in different ways, but the lawyer will earn perhaps ten times as much as the sweeper. Is this because one works with hands and other with brain? Is it because of the length of training? Is it because society needs one more than the other? Is it because of demand — anyone could sweep a road, but few could argue in a court of law? Should people be rewarded according to their value to the community — the farm worker on whom everyone depends for basic food being paid the most, and the pop-singer being paid least? How should wages be assessed in a just society?

Job satisfaction. Some people — writers, for example — often work twice the national average hours, and earn half the average wages. A doctor may work 80 or 90 hours a week — and get no extra money. Yet none of them would do any other job, because they enjoy what they are doing. The reward is partly in cash, partly in job satisfaction. While it is easy to see that some occupations can be rewarding in themselves, how can such tasks as working on an assembly line, repeating the same operation hundreds of times a day give any pleasure? Should society accept that some people are going to get enjoyment from work, and pay them less, while those who do the more unpleasant jobs, such as refuse collection or coal mining, should be paid more? Should people all be paid about the same and be placed in the jobs which they enjoy?

Self-respect, fellowship. Work has other attractions beside money and satisfaction. Many people enjoy the companionship of others, and the social life which comes from it. They enjoy working with a group and perhaps achieving something together. There can be a pride in the product — the best cars or jam tarts or newspaper. Work generally gives self-respect, and fulfils the basic human need to be wanted. A person in work has a role in life, whether it is as a high court judge, or serving in a bar. It is the loss of self-respect and a feeling that one is somehow inferior, and not the actual loss of income which many unemployed people say hurts them most.

UNEMPLOYMENT

Causes of unemployment

1. Technology — with modern equipment one person can produce more than 10 or 20 could with older machinery. Agriculture, transport, building as well as ordinary factories are very seriously affected by this.

2. Demand for some goods — especially heavy industries such as steel and coal which needed large numbers of workers — has fallen dramatically because of new materials and fuels such as oil and nuclear power.

3. Other countries, especially in Asia, are able to produce goods much more cheaply than Western nations so that factories here have to close. Examples are Japanese electronics, cars and cameras, Korean ships and Indian textiles.

4. Rise in population — high birth rates of the 1950s and 1960s (about 16 per 1 000 of the population) have meant many more adults seeking work. High immigration rates at the same time have also contributed.

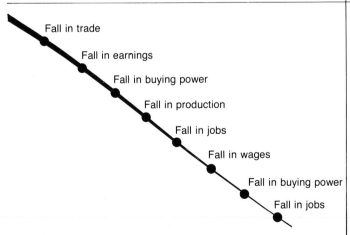

5. World recession and fall in trade in the 1980s has meant that people have less money to spend. This means they buy less, so that fewer goods are needed, which means factories close.

6. With some goods the market is almost saturated. Goods such as TVs, radios, washing machines, and refrigerators last for a long time, and when most homes have them the demand falls.

Effects of unemployment on the individual and the family

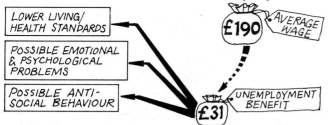

LOWER LIVING/ HEALTH STANDARDS

POSSIBLE EMOTIONAL & PSYCHOLOGICAL PROBLEMS

POSSIBLE ANTI-SOCIAL BEHAVIOUR

£190 AVERAGE WAGE

£31 UNEMPLOYMENT BENEFIT

Unemployment by occupation

MEN		
40%	semi/unskilled manual	(18%)
40%	skilled manual	(38%)
10%	clerical	(19%)
10%	managerial/professional	(25%)

WOMEN		
40%	semi/unskilled manual	(38%)
8%	skilled manual	(8%)
45%	clerical	(47%)
7%	managerial/professional	(7%)

0   40   80   90 100%

The figures in brackets show the percentage of the total work force in those occupations

Low income. The average income of a male manual worker (1986) was £190 a week. If he is unemployed this drops to £31 a week for a single person, £50 for a couple. If he still has no work after a year, the unemployment benefit stops, and he must apply for social security benefits. These will be higher, but will still be very far short of what he could earn in work. 40% of both unemployed men and women are unskilled or semi-skilled manual workers because these are the jobs that can be done most easily with new technology. Often these workers' wages were below average when they were in work, so that they had little chance to build up savings.

Emotional problems. Unemployed people often feel useless and rejected. They feel that they have failed and are unwanted, even though the unemployment is not their fault at all. There is a sense of loneliness and shame, and of being cut off from their friends who are still working. This can lead to physological problems and make them even less fitted for work if a job should be available.

This means the standard of life for the unemployed person and the family will fall. There could be less food, or food of cheaper, and perhaps less suitable, kinds. Clothing and household equipment will have to last longer. Holidays, entertainments and other luxuries will tend to disappear. Life will become much less pleasant, and at the very worst, poorer diet and clothing and lack of heating in winter could lead to medical problems.

Loss of incentive. When a person's life has had a routine — getting up, going to work, coming home etc — suddenly having nothing to do can have a dramatic effect. All incentive seems to go, and few can even make the effort to do jobs in the home that need doing — in any case, the shortage of money often means that they cannot afford the materials to do them. Boredom, resentment, frustration and anger often set in. This can lead to violence which shows itself as wife-beating or child-abuse in the home, or aggression and vandalism outside.

Crime rates can be higher among the unemployed. This is, of course, partly because of the need for money, but more, perhaps, because of boredom and the idea that any activity, even crime, gives them self-respect and standing among their companions.

Possible measures to help unemployment

1. Public works. The Government might employ people to do work which could be of long-term benefit to the country, such as making new roads, clearing slums, planting new forests, making parks and other leisure features. The money would have to come from taxes, of course, so that everyone would have to pay.

2. Shorter hours. If everyone worked less time, more people could be employed. If people worked only half time, two could be employed for each job, and with new equipment could probably produce twice as much. There would, of course, have to be two lots of wages instead of one, but this could be made up by the extra production (if the goods could be sold).

3. Earlier retirement. If people retired at 55 or even 50 there would be more jobs for younger people. The older people would have to have pensions much earlier than at present and this again would have to be paid by the taxpayers.

4. A movement to service industries. People have much more leisure today and with decreasing working hours will have more. More people could be employed in service industries such as hotel, restaurants, amusements, entertainment, sports facilities, etc. In some countries, especially America, this change is taking place rapidly.

5. Government might help to retrain people from older, dying industries for new ones such as computer programming or service industries. The Government could also give financial aid to help people to move to areas where there are jobs available, and also to enable people to set up their own employment.

6. Government money to subsidise decaying or over-manned industries such as steel making, mining and railways so that people not really needed could be kept in employment. If jobs are lost the Government has to pay unemployment benefit to those out of work. It might be better to pay them to keep them in work.

TRADE UNIONS

TABLE OF FINES (shillings)	
Any spinner found with his window open	— 1s
Any spinner found dirty at his work	— 1s
Any spinner found washing himself	— 1s
Any spinner with gaslight on too long	— 2s
Any spinner heard whistling	— 1s
Any spinner being five minutes late	— 1s
Any spinner being sick and cannot find another to give satisfaction must pay for steam per day	— 6s

The notice above shows just a few of the fines imposed on cotton workers in 1823. When a man's wages were rarely more than 10 shillings a week, he could often find himself at the end of a 6½ day week of 80+ hours, *owing* the owner money instead of receiving any wages. Conditions in the early factories were appalling and dangerous: women and children from the age of three worked underground in the coal mines; whenever trade was bad large numbers were dismissed without any compensation or unemployment pay. If people tried to get better wages, they were dismissed and new workers, who were only too willing to work for less, were employed. It is not surprising that workers tried to band together to improve the terrible conditions, but any such associations were illegal until 1825. Even when people were allowed to form trade unions, these were generally very weak, and could be easily defeated by the employers. The struggle of the unions to get power took over 50 years of industrial, political and legal battling.

Aims

A trade union is an association of members of one trade, or similar trades, to improve the conditions of *its own members.* It should be noted that improved wages or conditions for one set of workers can mean worse conditions for another: a very large wage rise for steel workers would mean an increase in the price of metal for the car industry. This would mean an increase in the price of new cars, so that people would keep their old ones longer — and unemployment in the car and component factories would result. The main aims of trade unions are:

1. Higher wages for their members. This may be achieved by a straight wage increase or by other methods such as bonus schemes or more overtime.

3. Legal protection for members in disputes with employers.

2. Better conditions, shorter hours of work, longer holidays.

4. Welfare of members — clubs, convalescent homes, help for widows and orphans, strike pay.

Achieving aims

Trade unions set out to achieve their aims by:

Negotiating — with the employers (collective bargaining).

Industrial action — strikes, working to rule, sympathetic strikes, picketing.

Recruiting — as many members as possible to increase their power. To do this they may insist on a 'closed shop' policy — that is, insist that everyone employed in that particular industry, or factory, *must* be a member of their, or an allied, trade union.

Changing laws —to meet their demands. Unions can do this because the Labour party is largely financed by contributions from union members. Some unions too sponsor MPs. When the Labour party is in power the unions can bring considerable pressure on the Government.

Organisation

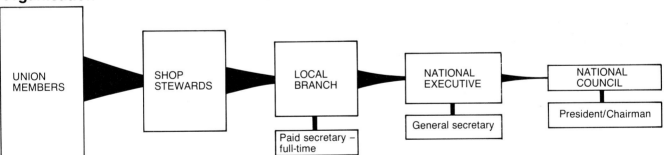

A typical union organisation is: (1) an elected National Council, with a president or chairman; (2) an elected National Executive with a General Secretary, who has immense power in the union and runs its day-to-day affairs; (3) local branches with a full-time secretary; (4) shop stewards in workplaces, sometimes full-time, sometimes part-time.

Trade unions fall roughly into three groups:

Professional, scientific, managerial
Association of Scientific, Technical and Managerial Staff (ASTMS); National Union of Teachers (NUT); Banking, Insurance and Finance Union; Musicians' Union; Hospital Consultants and Specialists Association.

Skilled workers
Electrical, Electronic, Telecommunication and Plumbing Union; Associated Society of Locomotive Engineers and Firemen (ASLEF) ; Iron and Steel Trades Confederation; Felt Hat Trimmers and Wool Formers.

Unskilled workers
National Union of Mineworkers (NUM); Shop, Distributive and Allied Workers; Transport and General Workers Union; National Union of Public Employees (NUPE).

SOME PROBLEMS WITHIN THE TRADE UNIONS

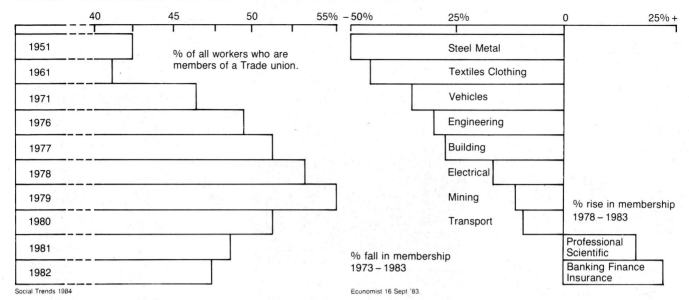

Left graph: % of all workers who are members of a Trade union. (scale 40, 45, 50, 55%)

1951
1961
1971
1976
1977
1978
1979
1980
1981
1982

Social Trends 1984

Right graph: scale −50%, 25%, 0, 25%+

Steel Metal
Textiles Clothing
Vehicles
Engineering
Building
Electrical
Mining
Transport
Professional Scientific
Banking Finance Insurance

% rise in membership 1978 – 1983

% fall in membership 1973 – 1983

Economist 16 Sept '83.

Over the last 100 years the trade unions have won many of the battles they were formed to fight. They have, of course, an essential role to play in any society, but today they have many problems. These are largely connected with the changing patterns of industry. The two graphs below show some of the basic problems of trade unions — the falling proportion of the working population who belong to a union, coupled with the decline in the older, heavy-industry unions and the rise of those for professional, scientific and clerical workers. These 'white collar' workers often have a reasonably high standard of living, and many of them considerable job-satisfaction, so that they are generally much less militant than unions of manual workers.

The new technology and other factors have caused world-wide unemployment. In times when work is scarce people are more likely to put loyalty to their family first, by keeping the jobs they have, rather than loyalty to a union, which would risk their income by going on strike. Some unions too are reluctant to accept new work techniques which they see as putting their members out of employment. Employers feel that the 'restrictive practices' which are used by some unions to try to keep jobs, merely increase costs and eventually lose more jobs than they keep — which weakens the union.

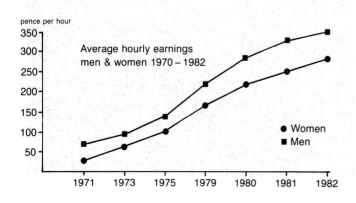

Average hourly earnings men & women 1970 – 1982

pence per hour (scale 50, 100, 150, 200, 250, 300, 350)

● Women
■ Men

(years: 1971, 1973, 1975, 1979, 1980, 1981, 1982)

The graphs show how average hourly earning of all workers rose between 1971 and 1984, mainly because of trade union efforts. Of course the much increased cost of living has to be taken into account, but the 'real' value of wages has risen by about 10% — which means a higher standard of living for most people. There were, for example, 12 million private cars in 1970, against 17 million in 1985.

On the other hand, it takes more man-hours to produce one Ford Escort in a British factory, than in a German one. In general, trade unions in Germany are less powerful than in Britain, but the workers are paid higher wages. Do you consider this a criticism of British trade unions — or British management?

INDUSTRIAL GROUPS

Trades Union Congress (TUC) is the 'parliament' of the movement. The unions send delegates to the annual TUC Conference, which elects a General Council — the 'cabinet'. There is a permanent General Secretary, who has great influence over industrial relations. The TUC coordinates the activities of most of the unions in Britain, and deals with the problems which concern them all. It gives help and advice to particular unions and industries; it has wide educational programmes, and keeps the Government informed of what it sees as industrial, social and economic issues.

Confederation of British Industry (CBI)
Employers too have their 'trade unions', the largest of which is the CBI. This represents 300 000 companies, private and nationalised, large and small, employing over half the workers in Britain. The aim of the CBI is to make sure that Government, the public and international organisations understand the needs and aims of business people. The CBI sends representatives to The National Economic Development Council, the Manpower Services Commission, and the Advisory, Conciliation and Arbitration Service.

National Economic Development Council. This is
an attempt to put economic and industrial problems above the separate interests of trade unions, employers, political parties or governments, and to do what is best for the country as a whole. The Council is made up of six cabinet ministers (including the Chancellor of the Exchequer), six senior trade union representatives, six members of the CBI, and four independent members. They exchange information and objectives, and try to get the different branches of the economy and industry to work together.

Advisory, Conciliation and Arbitration Service (ACAS)
is a committee made up of three members nominated by the TUC, three by the CBI and three independent members together with a chairman, which tries to settle disputes between employers and unions by negotiation rather than by industrial action. Both parties have to agree to the intervention of ACAS into a dispute, and neither party is bound to accept its decision.

LEISURE

The average adults' weekly time is divided roughly as shown in the chart. For at least half of the time they can do what they like — though of course there are meals, washing, dressing and odd jobs which are essential. But even so, approximately half of a normal working person's waking time is leisure, to be used as she or he wants. As a result of the great increase in unemployment during the past six years, millions of people have been forced to find leisure activities for all their working hours.

In the last 40 years there has been a marked increase in the amount of leisure activity, and in the kinds of activity available for most people. Some of the reasons are shown below.

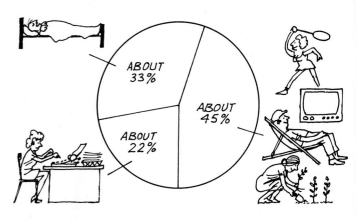

Much more free time. The working week is shorter, and labour-saving equipment and products have reduced house work to a minimum.

People are better off in real terms. There is more to spend on leisure activities — holidays, sports gear, radio and tv equipment and outside entertainment and sports.

Travel is quicker, easier and cheaper — private cars. Air travel allows people to have a week's holiday in places which would have a month to reach only a few years ago.

There are increasing facilities for leisure — leisure centres, parks, packaged holidays, and service industries in general. Technology has opened up new leisure fields — tv, videos, electronic games, sub-aqua equipment, hang-gliding etc.

The media shows us exciting places and activities and give advice on how to enjoy them. Health programmes and articles may start new leisures — jogging, for example.

MORE LEISURE

WIDER RANGE OF LEISURE ACTIVITIES

Broader education lets people know what activities there are for enjoyment — many new sports, crafts and other activities are introduced in schools, which people follow when they leave.

Advertising pressures — sports equipment, brochures for holidays, advertisements for leisure activities of all kinds can tempt us to spend more on leisure.

Rising expectations and standard of living. Everyone can now expect to enjoy some of the pleasure that once only the rich could afford — skiing, horse-riding, foreign travel, sailing, etc.

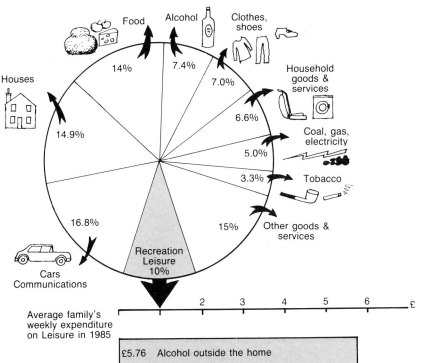

Government figures show that the average family spent £30 a week on leisure activities and materials in 1984 — about 16.5% of the total budget. Travelling costs which are normally part of leisure expenditure were not included: if these were added the price of leisure would probably be nearer 20-25%. The chart shows how this money is spent in a typical household.

Average family's weekly expenditure on Leisure in 1985

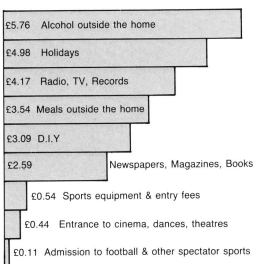

£5.76 Alcohol outside the home
£4.98 Holidays
£4.17 Radio, TV, Records
£3.54 Meals outside the home
£3.09 D.I.Y
£2.59 Newspapers, Magazines, Books
£0.54 Sports equipment & entry fees
£0.44 Entrance to cinema, dances, theatres
£0.11 Admission to football & other spectator sports

Because of the reasons shown on page 128, there has been a marked change in the pattern of leisure in the last 10 years, with a movement from spectator sports outside the home to domestic entertainment (TV, radio, video) and a steady increase in the amount of participant sports. The numbers attending football matches, racing and cinema are obviously much larger than those actually playing badminton or cycling for sport, and the diagram shows the percentage change between 1971 and 1982. The figures in brackets indicate the actual numbers involved in 1982.

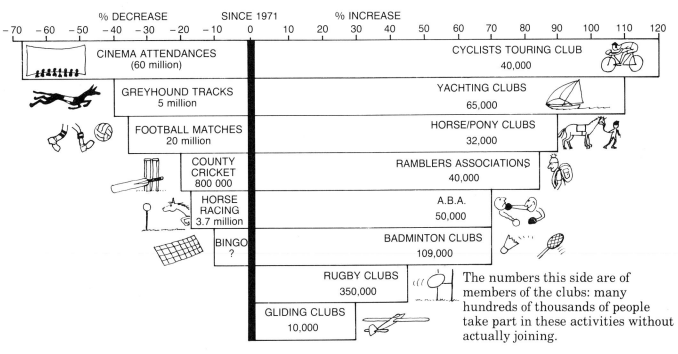

% DECREASE   SINCE 1971   % INCREASE

CINEMA ATTENDANCES (60 million) — CYCLISTS TOURING CLUB 40,000
GREYHOUND TRACKS 5 million — YACHTING CLUBS 65,000
FOOTBALL MATCHES 20 million — HORSE/PONY CLUBS 32,000
COUNTY CRICKET 800 000 — RAMBLERS ASSOCIATIONS 40,000
HORSE RACING 3.7 million — A.B.A. 50,000
BINGO ? — BADMINTON CLUBS 109,000
RUGBY CLUBS 350,000
GLIDING CLUBS 10,000

The numbers this side are of members of the clubs: many hundreds of thousands of people take part in these activities without actually joining.

Education for leisure

No one would dream of setting people to work in a factory or office to work for eight hours a day without some training, yet education for leisure, which can occupy up to 12 hours a day, is rarely considered. People can *fill* those hours, watching TV, playing electronic games, listening to records, and many other ways, but are these the best things? Of course the people will enjoy them or else they would not do them, but how do they know there are not things from which they would get far more pleasure?

With the working hours falling, and work itself often becoming less demanding as automation and electronic equipment take over, the need for education for leisure is becoming more urgent. This does not mean just telling people what they should enjoy, but showing them the great range of activities, active and passive, mental and physical, which are available, and how to get the maximum pleasure from the ones they choose.

Tackling the problem

How should this be done? Schools must, of course, continue to teach mathematics, languages, and other subjects which are essential to get the most out of any leisure activity, especially those which probably will take up the majority of spare time — TV, radio, newspapers and books. Many schools do offer a wide range of crafts and sports, but even the greatest enthusiast will find that in adult life these will take up only a very small part of recreational time. Should schools offer a wider range of 'sampler' activities from archaeology to zoology so that students can learn what is available? What would the practical and economic problems of such courses be? Should students be forced to take such courses, or be allowed to opt for those they choose? It must be remembered that the early stages of education for leisure, as for anything else, can be hard, boring or painful, but they do lead to a much greater enjoyment of that recreation later.

Or should schools provide just the basic background — as they do generally for work — and allow people to find their own favourite activities in adult life?

Adult education

One important way to learn about new leisure activities is the adult education scheme provided by all education authorities. One very small authority offers the following subjects as daytime or evening courses in its light craft section alone: painting, life painting, painting and composition, portrait painting, photography, pottery, design, printing, embroidery, lacemaking, patchwork, macrame, leatherwork, enamelling, pewter and copper work, silversmithing, wood carving, wood sculpture, weaving and dyeing, soft toy making, collage, crochet and knitting. Other sections are indoor sports, outdoor sports, academic subjects, languages and many others. Larger educational authorities offer a much wider range: the problem is how to get people to use the facilities available. Find out what courses your local authority offers.

Questions

Pollution and conservation

1. Pollution

Write an essay on pollution, use the following as a plan.

(a) What is meant by the term "pollution"? Give *two* examples.

(b) What are the effects of pollution on people and the surroundings in which they live? Use suitable examples to illustrate your answer.

(c) Describe some of the ways in which Government and other organisations have helped to reduce pollution in this country.

2. Pollution

"The earth is the platform we live on. The thin crust of soil sustains us with food. The thin layer of air is our oxygen tent.

Man has come to dominate the earth and to prosper by his cleverness. With the tools and technological knowledge now at his command, he not only tinkers with his environment to make it more comfortable — he rapes it. We continue, nevertheless, to use brute force to make natural resources yield up what we want — now — from them. Danger signals blink urgently on all sides. Our survival really is in the balance.

The world population explosion races ahead faster than all the improved techniques for growing food. We pollute the air with smoke and radiation. We use the oceans and rivers as drains for our bodily and industrial wastes. We poison 'pests' with chemical sprays, but other pests, which were kept in check by those killed off, swarm in unhampered. And we ultimately poison ourselves. We dump huge quantities of chemical fertilisers, mostly the DDT types, and pesticides such as aldrin, dieldrin and endrin, on the fields to help grow bigger and better crops; but the fertilizers wash into the lakes and rivers, where they kill off the fish and also stimulate bigger and better beds of weeds..."

("Silent Spring" — Rachel Carson)

(a) What are the three types of pollution mentioned in the text?

(b) Give one other example of a type of pollution.

(c) What does the author mean when she says that we poison ourselves when we apply fertiliser to the land?

(d) From your Social Studies work, say what we mean by the term "population explosion" and suggest solutions to this problem.

The world of work

3. Work and leisure

"Alienation exists when workers are unable to control their immediate work processes, to develop a sense of purpose and function which connects their jobs to the overall organisation of production, to belong to integrated industrial communities, and when they fail to become involved in the activity of work as a mode of personal self expression."

R Blauner 'Alienation & Freedom'

(a) Carefully explain what the author of this statement means by alienation from work.

(b) If work is so alienating why is mass unemployment so bad?

4. Work and leisure

Does the type of job determine the type of leisure?

5. Work

The information given below refers to the working population of Great Britain betwen June 1973 and June 1983.

Manpower and incomes			
	June 1973	June 1978	June 1983
Total working population as a percentage of population	25.6m 45.6%	26.3m 47.2%	26.7m 47.4%
Total employees in employment	22.6m	22.7m	21.1m
Wholly unemployed as a percentage of population	0.5m 2.2%	1.3m 5.1%	2.9m 11.2%
Industrial stoppages — working days lost	7.2m	9.4m	3.6m
Sickness — working days lost	319m	334m	372m
			m=millions

(a) (i) What was the total working population in June 1983?

  (ii) What percentage of the population was this?

(b) What percentage of the working population was unemployed in

  (i) June 1973?

  (ii) June 1983?

(c) (i) Using graph paper draw two graphs of (1) the total working population and (2) the total employees in employment from June 1973 to June 1983.

  (ii) Describe what happened between June 1973 to June 1983 to
  (1) the total working population.
  (2) the total employees in employment

6. Work and leisure

People today have more leisure time and money to spend on leisure. What leisure activities are available in Britain today and what sort of people participate in which activity?

7. Unemployment

"The only people who are unemployed are those who want to be. There are plenty of opportunities available if people are prepared to do different jobs in another part of the country". Discuss.

8. Trade unions

(a) What benefits do trade unions offer their members?

(b) What are the disadvantages of trade unions?

9. Pollution

(a) Give a definition of pollution.

(b) State *two* common examples of pollution and in each case name its source, the nature of the pollutant, and its effect on the environment and living organisms.

10. Pollution

Study the diagram below and answer the questions which follow:

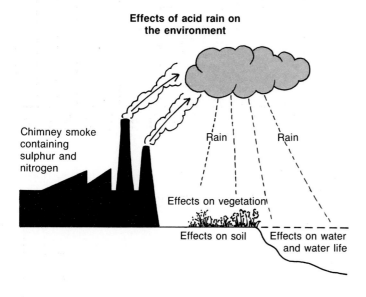

Effects of acid rain on the environment

Chimney smoke containing sulphur and nitrogen

Rain   Rain

Effects on vegetation

Effects on soil   Effects on water and water life

(a) What causes pollution in the above diagram?

(b) Name any *two* effects which acid rain has on the environment.

(c) Describe any *one* measure which could be taken to reduce the effects of acid rain.

(d) Describe and explain the effects of any *two* other forms of environmental pollution.

(e) Everybody thinks that pollution is a bad thing. Why do you think that it continues?

(f) Using examples, describe how pressure groups have tried to protect the environment.

Why are some pressure groups more successful than others?

11. Conservation

Study the following extract and answer the questions which follow.

SAVE THE AVON GORGE

In 1971 Bristol Corporation gave permission for a company to build a large hotel in the Avon Gorge, a steep-sided valley of outstanding natural beauty. The hotel was to be situated close to the famous and spectacular Clifton Suspension Bridge, built by Isambard K. Brunel in the nineteenth century.

The planning permission was discovered by a member of the local society concerned with preserving the character of the area. Without delay a meeting was called to discuss opposition to the scheme. It was attended by about twenty people, who called themselves STAG (Save the Avon Gorge). Local MPs were contacted, and questions asked in the Commons. The Minister for the Environment and the press were invited to investigate the matter, and posters and car stickers were distributed. Before long, letters of support were pouring in, and a petition was started. Various public figures were asked to help, and among others John Betjeman, the poet laureate, came to Bristol.

The Minister set up a public enquiry, conducted by a planning inspector. It opened in May 1971 and lasted nine days. Opposing the hotel scheme were the National Trust and various local councils, together with individual architects and engineers. On the other side were Bristol Corporation officials, hotel representatives and some architects. In October the Minister accepted the findings of the enquiry and permission to build the hotel was refused. STAG had won.

This case illustrates an important point about 'one issue' pressure groups. STAG won not so much because of the volume of public protest but because it managed to attract influential supporters. Most of its members were middle class, professional people, who knew how to organise themselves effectively and where to exert pressure.

(Source: British Government, Philip Gabriel, Longman)

(a) In what ways was pressure put on Parliament by STAG?

(b) In what other ways did STAG promote its cause?

(c) It was not so much the number of supporters that STAG had, it was the kind of supporters. Explain in your own words how this was so.

(d) What is a 'one issue' pressure group?

(e) What is another name for such a group?

(f) Apart from the 'one issue' pressure group, what other main type of pressure group is there? Give examples.

(g) "Pressure groups are the means whereby anyone in Britain can have their say and influence decisions made about life in Britain." Discuss this statement and include examples in your answer.

12. Work

"People only work for money"

(a) Explain the meaning of the term 'work'.

(b) List two occupations which can be considered work by some and leisure by others.

(c) Outline four different ways in which work can affect leisure.

(d) For what other reasons, apart from money, do people work?

13. Work

Study the information in Table A and then answer the questions which follow.

Table A **Percentage of Working Population in Britain who work in different sectors of the economy, 1950 compared with 1980.**

SECTOR OF THE ECONOMY	1950	1980
Primary industries (e.g. coal mining, agriculture)	10	5
Manufacturing industries	50	40
Service industries (e.g. banking, tourism)	40	55
	100	100

(i) Which sector of the economy has had the biggest *proportionate* change in employment between 1950 and 1980?

(ii) Explain why the proportion of people employed in manufacturing industries has dropped between 1950 and 1980.

14. Unemployment

Study the diagram, below and answer the questions which follow:

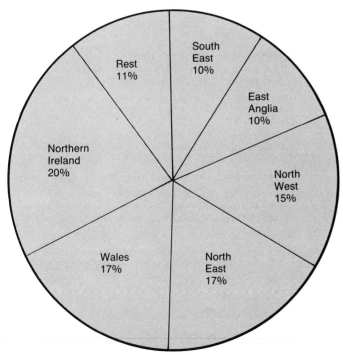

Unemployment in the UK by regions

(a) Which region in England has the highest unemployment rate?

(b) Why have some areas of the country been more affected by unemployment than others?

15. Unemployment

Study figures 1 and 2 below and answer the questions which follow:

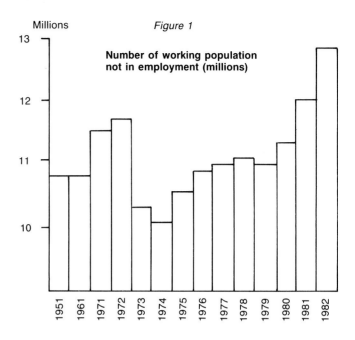

Figure 1

Millions

Number of working population not in employment (millions)

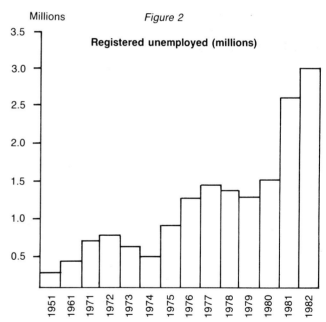

Figure 2

Millions

Registered unemployed (millions)

(a) Approximately how many of the "Working Population" were not in employment in 1982?

(b) Approximately how many people were registered as unemployed in 1982?

(c) Give *three* reasons why the number of Registered Unemployed (figure 2) is *less* than the number of Working Population Not in Employment (figure 1).

(d) Describe, with an example, the meaning of 'seasonal' unemployment.

(e) Describe, and explain, regional differences in the level of unemployment within the United Kingdom.

(f) How does unemployment affect individuals, families and communities?

TRADE AND INDUSTRY

It is almost impossible to think of anything we own that we have made *entirely* by ourselves, without help from anyone else. Perhaps father and his prize marrow is an exception.

Millions of people either directly of indirectly have helped father with his prize marrow. Take the simplest thing you have, and try to trace all the people who have had a hand in it before it reached you.

But what about: seed growers; foresters; paper, glue and ink makers; iron and coal mines; steel furnaces; tool manufacturers; transport of all kinds; oil wells; office staff; wholesalers; retailers; banks; insurance?...The list is endless.

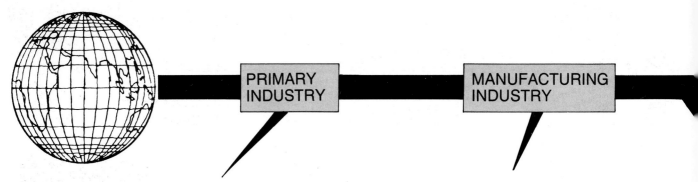

PRIMARY INDUSTRY

MANUFACTURING INDUSTRY

Primary industry:

Everything we use comes first of all as a natural product from the earth. The raw materials can be the products of farming, horticulture and fishing (food, leather, glues, some chemicals and medicines); of forestry (timber and wood products of all kinds, paper chemicals, rubber); of mines, quarries and oil wells (coal, iron, oil, cement, jewellery, chemicals and all minerals). The last group are sometimes called extractive industries because they are extracted from the earth. Primary industries of course draw heavily on manufacturing industries — machinery, chemicals, transport, etc.

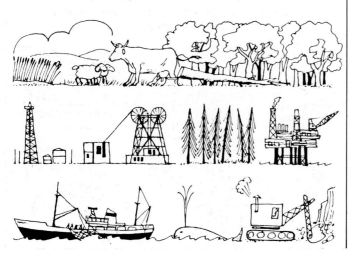

Manufacturing industry:

Takes the raw materials and turns them into all the things we want, from aspirins to zippers, and aeroplanes to zithers. Manufacturing industries take raw materials from many sources to turn them into the finished product: a tinned fruit factory needs the basic fruit from the orchards; sugar from sugar plantations; water; chemicals for preservatives and colour; iron for the tins; paper and printing for the labels, to say nothing of all the distribution services (transport of all kinds with their dependent industries) financial systems and so on.

Commerce:

Trade is the way the goods get from the people who produce them, either primary or manufacturing industries, to the people who use them (consumers). This involves buying, selling, dealing and exchanging raw materials and finished products, and all the associated clerical and financial work. The producer does not generally deal directly with the public, but sells to a wholesaler, who buys in very large quantities. The wholesaler sells to the retailer, who buys in smaller amounts, and the retailer sells to the consumer.

Aids to trade:

Trade and industry at every level needs many services. There are banking, insurance, stock exchanges, clerical work, credit operations, accountants, lawyers, postal and telephone services, transport, advertising, public relations, computers and so on. A complex commodity such as a motor must involve indirectly every kind of producer, manufacturing industry and aid to trade that exists.

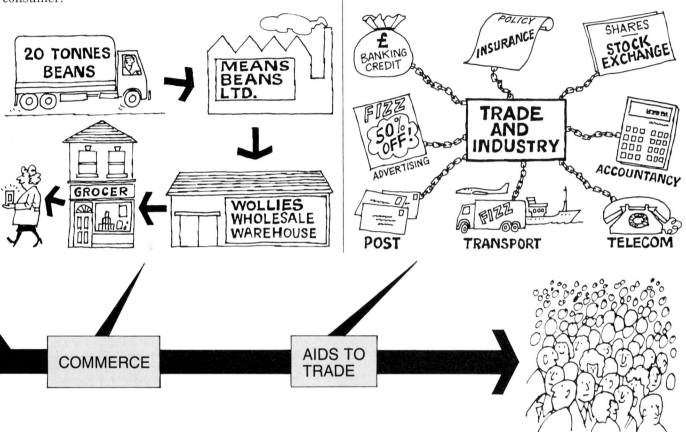

Direct services:

30% of all workers are not employed in industry, commerce or aids to trade. They do not have any direct effect on production or trade, but it would be impossible to run a modern state without them. They include doctors, dentists, nurses, teachers, policemen, lawyers, government officials, artists, entertainers, radio and TV workers, writers, musicians and professional sportspeople and so on. These are called direct services.

RETAILING
Supply and demand

Outside communist-controlled countries prices — and largely wages — are determined by the laws of supply and demand.

If many people want a certain article and there are few available, the seller can increase the price, knowing that if one person will not buy, there are plenty who will. High profits will attract other traders into that market.

If the demand for an article falls, either because there are plenty of them or it is not longer so desirable, the seller will have to reduce prices in order to try to attract customers. Prices may fall so low that some traders are forced out of business.

Now there will be a shortage again, and prices will rise though usually not as high as originally. Higher prices will attract more traders, and the prices fall again. This continues until a fairly steady price is reached.

Not many years ago many streets in towns looked like this, with many small shops selling one type of product — meat, fish, clothing, hardware.

Today many streets are more like this, with supermarkets, specialist chain shops, shopping precincts. Outside some towns hypermarkets have been opened.

Shopping precincts

Many towns have a traffic-free area, often specially built, where the majority of the shops, supermarkets and services such as banks and post offices are situated. Sometimes they are covered in and have air conditioning, play areas and decorative features such as gardens and statues. Usually there is a large car park adjacent.

Shopping precincts allow people to do most of their shopping safely in one area. Rents for the shops are, however, very high so that smaller specialist traders cannot afford them. As a result the large national chain stores with their restricted, quick-selling goods, dominate the precincts, so that they all seem alike no matter where they are.

Hypermarkets

These are supermarkets on a large scale. They often sell furniture, carpets, heavy household and electrical goods, garden and DIY material, and even petrol and cars as well as the more usual supermarket items. They sometimes have restaurants, play areas and other services. As they are generally situated outside towns, where land is cheaper, they can offer lower prices and car parking.

Because they offer such a huge range of goods, hypermarkets tend to give less choice and stick to popular, widely-advertised lines. There are few unusual items. Service is even more impersonal than in supermarkets.

Supermarkets

These are large stores which sell a wide range of goods — fruit, vegetables, flowers, meat, fish, foods of all kinds, bread, wines, stationery, toiletries and small household equipment under one roof.

People can do all of the weekly shopping in one air-conditioned shop, which often has a car park nearby.

Prices are often lower, especially on own-brand goods, because the supermarket can buy in such large quantities from manufacturers. Customers can pick their own fruit and vegetables instead of being served by an assistant, and can walk round comparing prices of different brands.

Supermarkets however, often have a limited variety of items, stocking mainly quick-selling popular goods. Service is impersonal, and few assistants know much about the products on sale. Service can be slow at the check-outs especially at busy times.

Specialist chain shops

Some firms have shops all over the country selling a more restricted range of goods. Examples are: Dixons (radio and TV, electrical goods for the home); Boots (medicines, toiletries and fancy goods); W H Smith (newspapers, magazines, books, records and stationery). Other specialist chains sell shoes, underwear, leather goods and furniture.

PRIVATE BUSINESS OWNERSHIP

Sole Trader

A sole trader is a business owned and managed by one person, though he/she may have paid assistants. These are often corner shops, cafés, newsagents etc.

Advantages

1. Easy to set up — the owner just starts trading.

2. Not a great amount of capital needed.

3. The owner takes all of the profits — if any.

Disadvantages

1. The owner often has to work very long hours.

2. There is unlimited liability — if the owner gets into debt his/her premises, home and belongings can be sold to pay the debtors.

3. Because little capital is involved there is often little scope for expansion.

Partnerships

Two or more people may get together to set up a business as a partnership. The agreement can be quite informal — they agree among themselves how much each shall contribute in money and work, and make up their own rules. Often however they do have a legal agreement. The business is called such names as 'Bumble and Blunder', 'Bumble and Company' or 'The Cheerful Caff'. They must not use the word 'limited'.

Advantages

1. More capital is available so that bigger projects can be started.

2. Work is shared by the partners.

3. Easy to form — few legal problems.

4. Losses are shared among all partners.

5. New ideas and approaches are possible.

Disadvantages

1. Possible disagreement among the partners.

2. Still not large amounts of capital available.

3. In most cases all partners are legally responsible for debts, so that all of their possessions can be sold to pay off debtors.

Private limited companies

To get more capital than partners can raise for big projects, businesses may become private limited companies. Any number of people can buy shares in the company if the directors approve them — shares cannot be bought by anyone on the Stock Exchange. The company must now add 'Limited' or 'Ltd' after its name.

Advantages

1. Private limited companies can raise much more capital for expansion or new projects than a partnership.

2. If the company gets into debt the amount that shareholders can be forced to pay is limited to the amount that they invested — hence the word 'limited'.

Disadvantages

1. Private limited companies are expensive to set up, and involve a great deal of costly legal agreements.

2. Very carefully audited accounts must be kept by law. This can be expensive.

Co-operatives

A large number of people may get together to form a Co-operative Society. Each person buys a number of £1 shares — often only one. The money is used to set up a business. The shareholders elect a board of managers who must be members but need not have any business qualifications. The board chooses a professional business person to run the business on a day to day basis, but all major policy decisions are made by the board.

After all expenses have been paid the profits of the trading are shared among members on the basis of how much they have bought at the store — dividend. Today more often members are given stamps to stick on a card which can be redeemed for cash.

Advantages

1. Competitive prices, especially with own brand goods made in Co-op factories.

2. Dividends makes prices even more reasonable.

Disadvantages

1. Co-ops sometimes do not stock many national brands, and their own-label goods are not always liked.

2. Management by amateurs may not always be efficient.

Public Limited Companies (PLC)

If a company becomes very prosperous, or wishes to start an extremely expensive operation such as building a new factory or explore for oil underwater, it may need much more money than even a private limited company can raise. In this case it will 'go public' — that is, it will advertise for members of the public to buy shares in it on the stock exchanges. It may have millions of shareholders.

Because of the vast amounts of money involved and the great scope for fraud, public limited companies are very strictly controlled by law at every stage.

Advantages

1. Vast sums of money can be available for huge projects, such as building a channel tunnel for example, which no ordinary company could afford.

2. Shareholders liabilities in debt are limited to the amount of their original shares.

3. Shareholders can exercise some control over the management of the business by voting at the annual meeting of shareholders.

Disadvantages

1. PLCs are extremely expensive to set up — the cost of floating such a company could be several million pounds.

2. The companies are so big that they can become impersonal, inflexible and inefficient, employing far too many people.

3. Company records which the management would often like to be kept secret, must be available to the public.

PUBLIC BUSINESS OWNERSHIP

Some industries and services which are very important to the country as a whole are now run by the State. Most of these, like the railways and coal mines, once belonged to private companies, but because of changing demands were unable to make enough profit. Because the Government felt that in the public interest they should be kept going, they were Nationalised — that is, they were taken over and run by the State.

Nationalised industries and public corporations

British Rail. Post Office. National Coal Board. BBC/ITA. British Steel. British Ship Builders. **Bank of England.** Central Electricity Generating Board.
UK Atomic Energy Authority. British Waterways. Port of London Authority. British Tourist Authority. British National Oil Corporation.

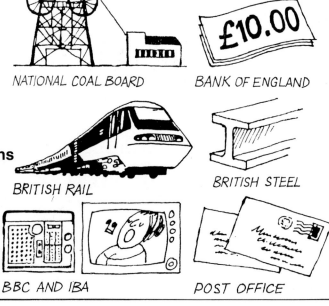

NATIONAL COAL BOARD

BANK OF ENGLAND

BRITISH RAIL

BRITISH STEEL

BBC AND IBA

POST OFFICE

Sometimes the Government has some control over an industry by buying a large number of shares in a private company on the stock market. In the case of some firms such as Austin Rover, it has a controlling interest (51%) of the shares.

Direct services. The government has a few industries which it controls directly for its own use.

AUSTIN ROVER

BP

HM STATIONERY OFFICE

SURVEY REPORT
REPORT
HANSARD
REPORT
STUDY
SURVEY

THE ROYAL MINT

How the state controls public enterprises

The appropriate government minister (transport, energy, trade and industry, postmaster general) who is responsible to Parliament, appoints the chairman of the board or corporation which runs each enterprise. The chairmen, with government approval, appoint members to the boards. The minister gives the boards a broad outline of how that particular enterprise is to be run, but allows them a free hand in the day-to-day management. The ministers can also, with government approval, give large sums of public money to the enterprises to cover losses or to finance development. In 1985 the National Coal Board made a loss of £875 million, and British Rail, made a loss of £235 million.

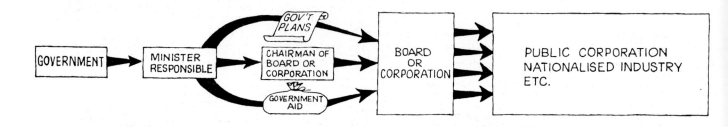

GOVERNMENT → MINISTER RESPONSIBLE → GOV'T PLANS / CHAIRMAN OF BOARD OR CORPORATION / GOVERNMENT AID → BOARD OR CORPORATION → PUBLIC CORPORATION NATIONALISED INDUSTRY ETC.

Nationalisation and de-nationalisation

An important difference between the Labour and Conservative parties is their attitude to nationalisation.

NATIONALISATION BALANCE

Labour

1. Services and industries which are vital to the State should be owned and run by the State, even if they make huge losses.

2. Enterprises run by private individuals or companies are interested only in making profits, so that the quality of goods and services are reduced, or prices increased, in order to make more money.

3. More important enterprises, such as banking and insurance, should be nationalised. Each of the major banks in Britain for example make about £500 million profit a year. If these were nationalised the money would go to the Treasury, and result in better schools, hospitals, roads, defence and so on.

Conservative

1. Some services which are unlikely ever to make enough profit for private companies but which are essential to the country (e.g. British Rail), should be left as nationalised industries.

2. National enterprises run by civil servants can become slow, over-staffed and inefficient because they have no competition. They feel that the Government is always there to hand out more money whatever their losses. Competition would make the enterprises more efficient.

3. There should be less nationalisation, and some state enterprises should be turned back into private companies by selling shares in them on the stock market. The Conservative Government since 1979 has denationalised: Britoil, Cable and Wireless, British Telecom, British Airways, the Gas industry, BAA and Rolls Royce, among others.

MORE   LESS

Municipal enterprises

Some town, city and county councils run enterprises of their own. Sometimes these are run as a service to the community, sometimes as modest profit earners to help the rates. Typical of municipal enterprises are: golf courses; restaurants; theatres; boating lakes; swimming pools; conference halls; seaside piers.

FINANCIAL INSTITUTIONS

It used to be said that love makes the world go round; in reality it is more likely that it is money that makes it turn.

Today almost everyone exchanges their labour or skills for money; then they exchange money for the things they want or need. As money is so important a whole industry has grown up to manage it.

Banks

Banks have four main functions:

1. To store our money safely until we need it.

2. To lend us money if we need it — and charge interest on the loan.

3. To offer us services such as cheques, credit cards, exchanging foreign currency, giving financial advice.

4. To make a profit for themselves and their shareholders.

Banks use the money that people have deposited with them to invest in the stock market. They make huge profits for their shareholders: from their investments; from the interest they charge on loans; the charges for the services they offer.

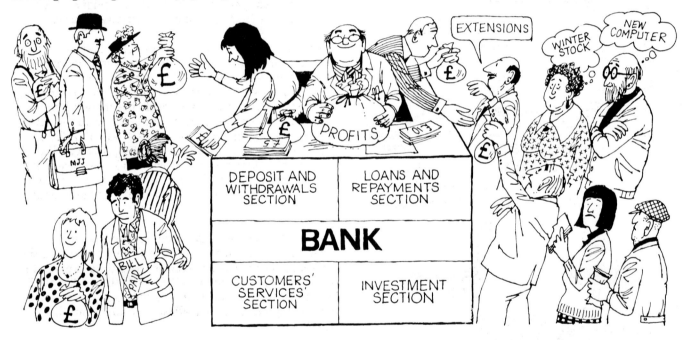

Insurance

Everyone is liable to have accidents or misfortunes which result in having to pay out more money than can be afforded. To cover this cost people take out insurances.

The insurance company promises in a legal document called a *policy* that they will pay a certain sum of money if their client suffers misfortune or loss in certain circumstances. The client agrees to pay the insurance company an amount of money (*premium*) every month or year.

Insurance can be taken out for almost anything:

having twins; bad weather on holiday, etc — but the most common are:

fire; accidents; floods; storm damage; theft; violence; carelessness by workpeople; life.

If an accident does not happen the insurance company keeps the premiums: if it does they pay out the sum agreed. In the case of life insurance (assurance) the money is paid to the person named in the policy — usually the next of kin.

The insurance company considers the risk involved before deciding on the premium a person will have to pay. A person living in a thatched house would pay more fire insurance than one living in one with a tiled roof. A person who lives in a city would pay more car insurance than one living in the country.

The insurance company makes its profits by balancing the risks and making sure that all the premiums paid in will be more than the money paid out.

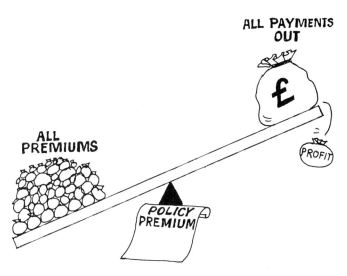

Building societies

The most expensive thing that most people buy in their lives is their house. Very few can afford to pay for it on the spot, and have to borrow money from a bank but most people do this from a society which specialises in lending money for buying houses.

Building societies take in money from investors, and pay them interest at about 9%. Some of this money they put in very safe investments, but much of it they lend to people wanting to borrow to buy homes. The borrowers agree to pay back the money by monthly instalments over a number of years — often 25. The borrowers also pay interest (about 12%) on the money still owing to the building society. The agreement between the borrower and the society is called a *mortgage*. If the borrowers cannot pay back their loan, the building society can take their house and sell it.

The building society makes some profit on its investments, and more on the difference between the interest it takes from borrowers and that it gives to its lenders. All of this profit is used to pay for staff, buildings and general running of the organisation — a building society is not allowed to make profit for itself.

Stock exchanges

These are institutions found in the largest cities where shares are bought and sold. People buy shares for several reasons:

1. To get an income from the dividends paid by the company each year.

2. In the hope of making a profit by buying the shares when they are cheap and selling when they are more expensive.

3. To protect their capital — the value of their shares goes up with inflation.

People with money to invest approach Market Makers either directly or through a bank or solicitor, and ask them to buy certain shares. The Market Manager goes to the Stock Exchange and tries to get the shares as cheaply as possible from other Market Makers whose clients have told them to sell. If they are successful they hand the document giving ownership of the shares to the client, and charge a commission for their work. The Market Makers handle sale of shares in the same way.

INFLATION

Inflation means a steep increase in the price of all goods and services. It is caused by a number of factors which are often related.

Inflation works in a spiral, forcing prices/wages/ profits higher and higher. This is particularly serious for countries like Britain which are dependent on exports. If the price of goods they sell abroad keeps rising, the buyers will look to other countries for their supplies, or set up factories of their own.

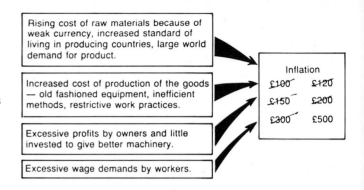

Once inflation has begun it is difficult to stop. Somehow governments have to break the spiral. Some of the ways of doing this are:

1. Freezing prices — if prices do not rise, there is no excuse for demanding higher wages and profits.

2. Freezing wages and profits — if production costs do not rise, there is no reason for higher prices.

3. Increasing efficiency in manufacturing — if each worker produces more, there is no reason for higher prices.

Unfortunately it is difficult for governments to impose any of these solutions effectively.

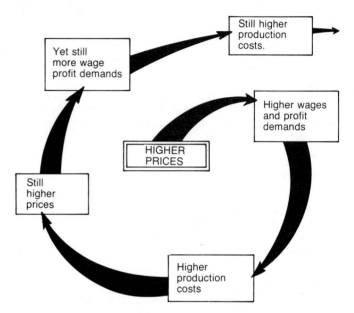

The money-go-round

Money is not much good unless we do something useful with it, such as buying things we want or investing it. If we hide it under the mattress, as some people used to, it just falls in value if there is any inflation. For example, if we had £10 in 1961 we could buy about 25 large paperback books with it. If however we hid it until 1987 and then spent it, we would be able to buy only 3 of the same paperbacks.

Until recently (until 1960 all wages, but not salaries, had by law to be paid in cash) the money-go-round worked rather like this.

Today more and more workers are paid by cheque or credits to the bank, and the bank sits at the centre of the financial roundabout.

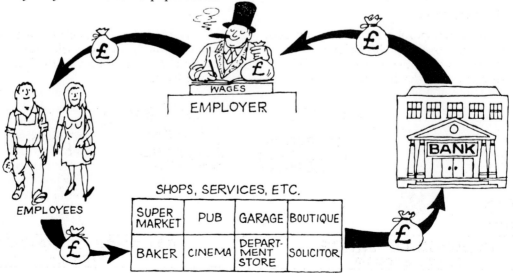

BALANCE OF TRADE

International trade

If people or countries earn more than they spend, either because they have a very high income or because they do not spend very much, they build up large surpluses in their banks and investments.

If they spend far more than they earn, either because their income is low or because they are extravagant, they become poor, get into debt or even become bankrupt.

Britain is a small, overcrowded country and cannot produce enough basic necessities, let alone luxuries for all the people. She must make a living by manufacturing goods for sale abroad. With the profits she can buy the raw materials for manufacturers and also the things such as food and textile she needs.

Britain's exports fall into two groups:

Visible exports

Apart from North Sea oil, these are all manufacturers: such as engineering and chemical products, textiles, cement, fertilisers, aeroplanes, ships, railways, oil, cars and lorries, electronic equipment.

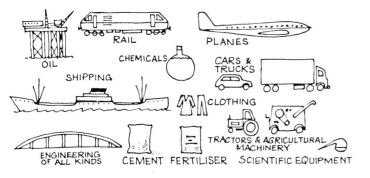

Invisible exports

These are *services* which are sold to other countries. They include: banking, insurances, tourism, freight charges on ships and aircraft, dividends from foreign investments.

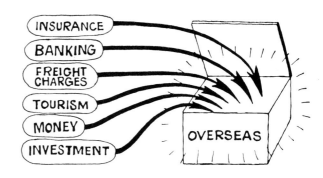

Balance of payments

For a country to be prosperous it must *export* more than it *imports*. This is called the *balance of payments*. Britain established a large 'invisible' market because she was the first country to become industrialised. London is still one of the largest financial centres in the world. The value of this 'invisible' trade is shown in the balance of payments figures for 1979.

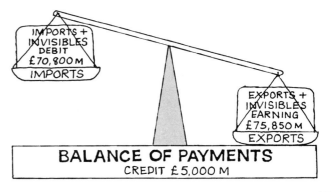

The developing countries

THE 'THIRD WORLD'

After World War II the great nations divided into two hostile groups — the communist states and the western 'democratic' states. Many countries in Asia, Africa and the Middle East did not want to be tied to either group, and possibly get drawn into another war. In 1955 a conference of these 'non-aligned' nations met in Bandung, Indonesia. It was attended by 29 countries, all poor and under-developed, who became known as the Third World as opposed to the 'worlds' of communism and western 'democracy'. Soon they were joined by Latin American nations and states newly de-colonised in Asia and Africa, all of whom had similar problems.

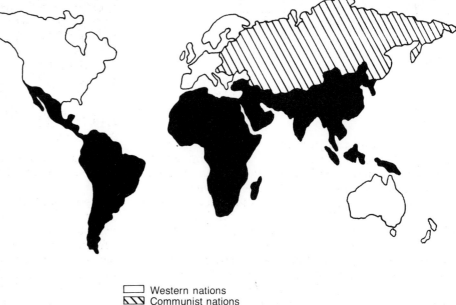

☐ Western nations
▨ Communist nations
■ Third world

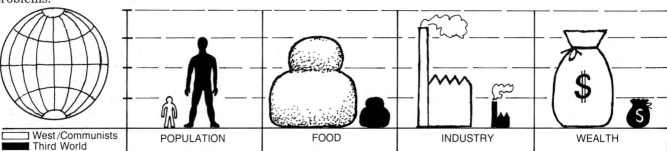

☐ West/Communists
■ Third World

POPULATION   FOOD   INDUSTRY   WEALTH

Feeding the poor in El Salvador

Problems of the developing countries

These photographs underline the basic problems of the Third World. They are:

1. Over population and desperate poverty.
2. Little industry and often few natural resources.
3. Disease, poor medical and health care.
4. Poor agriculture and starvation.
5. Few educational facilities and trained people.

Poverty and starvation in desert regions

NIGERIA 90%	
PAKISTAN 87%	
COLOMBIA 65%	
MEXICO 62%	
BRAZIL 57%	
INDIA 48%	
CHINA 47%	
USA 22%	
USSR 19%	
FRANCE 17%	
W.GERMANY 9%	
UK 5%	

% increase in population
between 1963 – 83
☐ Third world ☐ West/Comm.

Slum dwellers in Peru

Over-population and poverty

Three quarters of all the people in the world live in the developing countries, and their number is increasing dramatically. In the past people in the developing countries had very large families to compensate for the terrible number of child deaths, so that at least some would grow into adults. Today improved medical help (largely provided by the richer countries) has reduced the infant death rate, so that many more children survive, but the birth rate has not fallen. The next generation in turn have very large families. Worldwide campaigns by organisations such as WHO have reduced deaths from such diseases as cholera and smallpox, so that even though medical standards in the developing countries are very low, many more adults survive to add to the population explosion.

The poor land, even if farmed efficiently, which it often is not, could not possibly support so many people; there is little industry; great ignorance of how to cope with life under the bad conditions; and the result is great poverty. A typical labourer in a poor country might earn £15-£20 a month, compared with about £600 in Britain, or £750 in the United States. Even if the Third World peasant does not have nearly so much to pay out because standards of life are so different, there is still a great gulf between the two.

Poor agriculture, starvation

Much of the developing world is poor agricultural land (desert, mountains, swamps, or jungle) and many parts have a climate which is unsuitable for good farming — either too much rain (as in parts of Africa and South America) or not enough (great deserts in Africa, the Middle East and Asia). Farming methods are often very poor — small and uneconomic family plots cultivated with primitive hand tools. Seed is often of very poor low-yielding varieties very liable to diseases. The slash-and-burn technique and heavy grazing which were all right when there were only a few people who could move on when one area was exhausted are often still used. The deserts are growing at the rate of 50 000 square kilometres a year (an area larger than Switzerland). In many places livestock are hard to rear because there is not enough water, or because of insect-borne diseases. Much of the farming is subsistence — that is, the farmer grows just enough to keep his family alive, and when there is a bad harvest he has to borrow money for food and seed. This means that most of the

Lack of water in Kenya

Primitive agriculture in Indonesia

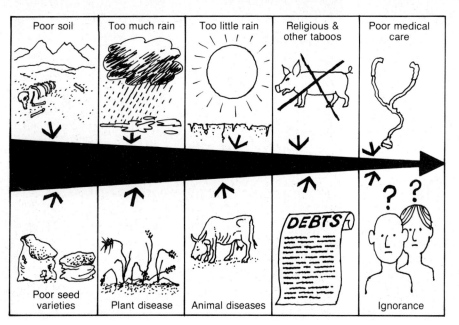

Poor soil | Too much rain | Too little rain | Religious & other taboos | Poor medical care

Poor seed varieties | Plant disease | Animal diseases | DEBTS | Ignorance

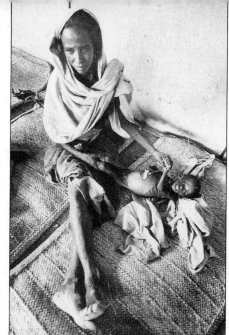

following year's crop is already pledged to pay back the loan and interest — which means more borrowing.

In some of the richer areas the best land is used to grow cash crops for export — tea, cotton, rubber, cocoa — which bring a great deal of money to the city merchants, but leaves the peasant farmer little better off as he has to buy food.

In the best years the land produces little more than enough to keep the family alive. A poor harvest or the death of an animal can mean disaster: the diet, always poor and very short of protein, falls to starvation levels. Sometimes religious or traditional customs forbid people to eat food which is available — certain animals, for example. At other times it is just ignorance which prevents people from using plants and other substances which are highly nutritious and in abundance. Tens of thousands of people, especially children, already weakened by bad feeding and poor conditions, fall easy victims to diseases. Medical resources, which are generally inadequate at the best of times, are completely unable to cope with the situation.

Lack of industry

Many developing countries have no large resources of industrial raw materials such as coal, metal ores and other minerals. Where they have, these are often difficult to get out because of lack of communications — roads and rail — but more because the country lacks the money to develop them. Richer nations have invested capital in some Third World countries to develop industry and mining, and have had many problems. There is a great shortage of trained labour, especially engineers and technoligists; there is much corruption, and money poured into the country for development vanishes into private pockets; there are rebellions or frequent changes of leader, and seizure by the Government which resents having outsiders to run their industry. As a result much of the important industries which would raise the standard of living is inefficient and corrupt, and much of its profits go into the hands of a few extremely wealthy people — who as often as not, are the country's leading politicians.

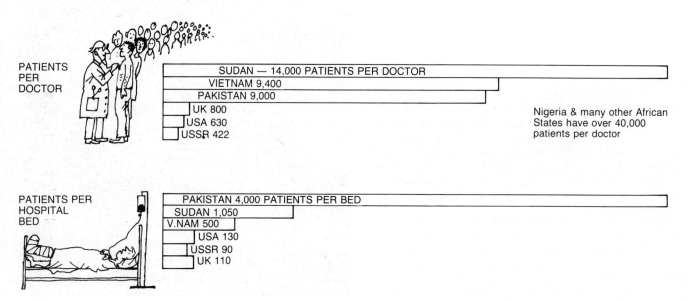

PATIENTS PER DOCTOR

SUDAN — 14,000 PATIENTS PER DOCTOR
VIETNAM 9,400
PAKISTAN 9,000
UK 800
USA 630
USSR 422

Nigeria & many other African States have over 40,000 patients per doctor

PATIENTS PER HOSPITAL BED

PAKISTAN 4,000 PATIENTS PER BED
SUDAN 1,050
V.NAM 500
USA 130
USSR 90
UK 110

Disease, poor medical and health care

The average expectation of life at birth in the West is about 71 for males and 76 for females: in many developing countries the figures are little more than half this. Malnutrition (often the wrong kind of food rather than insufficient) and ignorance of the simplest health precautions often makes diseases, which are fairly mild elsewhere, fatal in the developing countries. And on top of these, tropical countries have lethal diseases of their own. Everything is made worse in many places by the lack of clean water — the local stream or pool is often the village water supply, the village laundry, the local animal drinking and cleaning place, and the village sewage system. Water-borne diseases abound in the warm, filthy water, which also breeds countless insects which carry such illnesses as malaria and sleeping sickness.

Much of the medicine in the countryside is traditional folk and herbal remedies, mixed with magic, none of which is very effective against the virulent diseases of tropical countries. Even if an illness is diagnosed, the chances of the patient getting into a hospital, which is usually in a large town are very remote: the chart shows the number of doctors and hospital beds available for every 80 000 people.

These actual numbers do not show the standard of the doctor who in many developing countries has had only very limited training, often little more than first aid. Hospitals are often very primitive with several patients to a bed, and with the family present to cook and look after the sick person.

Lack of educational and training facilities

Many developing countries have very poor educational systems: schooling is often not compulsory, and in any case for the vast majority it does not go beyond a very low primary level. In the countryside where most people live, children are too valuable working on the land for them to spend much time in school. The State can afford little for its education, which means poor teachers, poor schools, few books and materials.

At secondary levels and above the situation is even more difficult, especially in professional and technical education, which is frequently geared to a particular political party line. The chart shows the number of scientists and technicians in the population of several eastern, western and developing countries.

Needs of the developing countries

Money. Money is the most important of all. The countries need it to finance agriculture, industry, education, health and communications. Countries can get loans from UN agencies or aid from other nations. They can also get private companies to invest in them. They have to remember that loans have to be repaid, even if at low interest rates, and that private investors will not put money into a business they think will not be profitable.

Education. To get a literate population which can be trained in higher skills a good basic education is essential. This is expensive, and it is a long time before results can be seen — and in any case teachers have to be trained before they can train pupils. Adults too need education to teach them elementary health and working methods as their own traditional ones are often very inefficient.

Expertise. Developing countries have few trained people, especially in the higher ranks of industry, science and commerce. They often hire foreign experts at high wages — or else manage with local people who are not up to international standards. The third world nations do not generally have a good primary and secondary school system, which can feed people into higher education quickly.

Voluntary organisations in developing countries

There are many voluntary organisations which try to help developing countries, sometimes on a short-term basis (when disasters such as famine or floods occur), and sometimes as longer-term projects. They may not have the vast funds of the international agencies but they are more flexible. They can pinpoint small, though vitally important areas and work on these with outstanding results.

1. Religious bodies of all faiths and creeds are particularly interested in education and medical care as long-term projects. Many leaders of the Third World countries began their education in mission schools: millions of third world people would not be alive today if it had not been for mission hospitals and teachers of child care.

2. Save the Children Fund deals entirely with problems of children. They run hospitals, clinics and orphanages: they have large immunisation and community health programmes; they train local people as basic health care nurses.

3. Oxfam, Christian Aid and a number of other organisations deal with problems that arise: emergency food, shelter and clothing in disasters; and more permanent projects such as digging wells, building schools and clinics, basic health care, teaching farming and other skills.

Health. Medical standards are rising, often with foreign help, and more children are surviving. This results in a population explosion (page xx). This increasing population more than offsets any improvement in agriculture and Family Planning is essential, but many of the poorest countries, especially in Latin America, are very strongly Catholic and are forbidden to practice reliable methods of birth control.

Markets. It is no use growing more crops or making new products unless they can be sold. Often third world farmers carry on growing crops which are of poor quality or else not needed elsewhere. Industrial products too are often crude, and not suited for sophisticated developed markets. Management and selling are skilled jobs, which again means education and training.

Political stability and honesty. Many third world countries have had rapid changes in leadership and political policy. There has been much corruption, and millions of pounds of aid have been stolen by high officials. Even if leaders are honest, they often do not have the right priorities, and set up expensive projects to make themselves popular with the people, or spend most of their aid on armaments to boost their own images.

Aid or trade?

If we imagine a starving, penniless family with a large uncultivated garden, we can help them either by giving them food, or by giving them tools, seeds and fertilisers so that they can keep themselves. Preferably, of course, we must give them some food while their own is growing. It is much the same with the third world. Often large sums of money sent as aid or loans is not used to the best advantage — on immediate 'wants' rather than future 'needs'. Lavish new capital cities and impressive military forces are all very well, but the needs of a sound economy, with good agriculture, growing industry, education and a decent standard of living (proper housing, water and power supplies, etc) for the people must be the first requirements. A good communications network is also essential.

It is understandable that the leaders and the people of the third world want immediately the kind of life they know exists in the developed countries. But this standard of living has taken hundreds of years to develop. It can come much more quickly in the third world because we now know how to achieve it, but it will still take time and may involve sacrifices for a while.

The developed countries can help at first by loans or aid and expert advice, and then by encouraging trade and not imposing tariff barriers.

Some features of the British economy

1. Trade and industry

Study the following list of twelve items. Then fill in the numbered boxes in the table below with the correct items under the different headings.

(a) Italian washing machine bought by housewife in Britain.
(b) British car sold in France
(c) British tourist in Greece
(d) Dutch tulips sold in English shops.
(e) British coal sold in France.
(f) British computer used in Germany.
(g) British washing machine bought by housewife in Italy.
(h) Spanish tourist in England.
(i) A Greek ship carries British goods.
(j) French apples sold in Britain.
(k) British insurance company insures an Italian ship.
(l) Belgian beer sold in Britain.

TOTAL EXPORTS

Visible	Invisible
1	5
2	6
3	
4	

TOTAL IMPORTS

Visible	Invisible
7	11
8	12
9	
10	

2. Trade and industry

Fill in the spaces in the following passage so that the whole passage makes sense.

When goods are brought into Great Britain from abroad they are known as .... Some of these goods are used to make other goods which may be sent back abroad, to be sold in a foreign country, and these are called .... The difference in value between the goods received from abroad and the goods sent abroad is known (on the Balance of Payments) as the ....

3. Trade and industry

The total value of all goods sold in a trading period is called
(a) gross profit
(b) total mark up
(c) turnover
(d) net profit

4. Retailing

What is the name of the type of retail outlet which sells products through catalogues and advertisements?

5. Retailing

A retail co-operative society passes on part of its profits to
(a) its employees
(b) its management
(c) its customers
(d) its suppliers

6. Retailing

(a) Name and describe *three* types of retail outlet and *one* type of wholesale outlet which use their own label brands.
(b) Explain *two* advantages and *one* disadvantage to the retailer of stocking their own label brands.
(c) Explain *one* advantage and *one* disadvantage to a manufacturer of supplying own label brands to retail organizations.

7. Business ownership

A sole trader
(a) has unlimited liability
(b) is the only person who works in a small retail business
(c) can have as many partners as he likes
(d) can sell shares to raise extra finance

8. Business ownership

A limited company obtains its issued capital from
(a) finance houses
(b) commercial banks
(c) stockbrokers
(d) shareholders

9. Business ownership

Which of the following organisations is part of public enterprise?
(a) Imperial Chemical Industries
(b) National Westminster Bank
(c) British Broadcasting Corporation
(d) The Rover Group

10. Business ownership

Study the four photographs labelled (A), (B), (C) and (D).

(a) Which of the business units shown in the photographs is most likely to be a partnership? Give your reasons.

(b) Which of the business units shown in the photographs is a public limited company?

(c) In which of the four business units will an owner have limited liability? Give your reasons.

(d) (i) What unit of ownership is (A) likely to be? Give your reasons. (ii) Explain how (A) is different from the other examples given.

11. Business ownership

Mr. Black operates an Estate Agency business in partnership with Mr. Brown. The main aim is to find buyers for their clients' properties.

(a) Describe *two* advantages to Mr. Black of operating this business as a partnership, rather than being in business as a sole trader.

(b) Does this business provide goods or a service? Give reasons for your answer.

Because of the large number of Estate Agencies in their area, the partners are considering the use of marketing methods as a means of competition.

(c) Explain what is meant by the term "marketing".

(b) Explain how *three* marketing methods could be used by the partners in competing with their rival Estate Agencies.

The partners have been offered the chance to join a national computer linked chain of Estate Agents. Details of property for sale would be held on a central computer and available through any of the offices nationwide. This would increase the capital employed but the partners hope the turnover would also be increased.

(e) Explain the terms "capital employed" and "turnover" as used above.

(f) Explain *two* advantages of using this computer system for the partners in their business and *one* way their customers would benefit from the change.

12. Business ownership

Mr. Green is the sole proprietor of a small engineering business. His balance sheet includes the following assets and liabilities:

MR. GREEN
Balance Sheet as at 31st December 1984

	£		£
Premises	10 000	Proprietor's	
Machinery	16 000	Capital	26 000
Vehicle	3 000	Long term loan	5 000
Stock	5 000	Trade creditors	9 000
Trade debtors	5 000		
Cash	1 000		
	40 000		40 000

(a) Give *one* example of an asset and *one* example of a liability from this balance sheet.

(b) Explain the meaning of:
    (i) "Proprietor's Capital";
    (ii) "Trade Creditors".

Mr. Green has been offered a small computer system for £10 000 which will enable him to increase the efficiency of his business.

(c) Describe *two* sources of finance which could be available to this sole proprietorship for the purpose of obtaining the computer system.

(d) Explain *two* advantages to Mr. Green of forming a private company.

13. Financial institutions

A payment made to a Girobank account holder by a person who does not have a Girobank account, must be made on the following form.

(a) credit transfer

(b) transcash

(c) giro credit

(d) girocheque

14. Financial institutions

A standing order is

(a) a regular amount paid into a current account

(b) a regular amount paid into a deposit account

(c) a regular payment out of a deposit account

(d) a regular payment out of a current account

15. Financial institutions

(a) Name the type of bank account that a person needs to have in order to be able to issue cheques.

(b) What is the name of the bank operated by the Post Office?

The developing countries

16. Problems of developing countries

"A typical diet which is essential for good health, should contain adequate quantities of proteins, carbohydrates, fats and vitamins".

(a) From the information supplied in the diagram say which parts of a "balanced diet" are insufficiently provided in India.

(b) How do such shortages affect the lives of the people in India?

(c) Explain why such gaps in living standards exist between rich and poor nations.

(d) What steps can be taken to deal with the problems of poorer nations?

The daily diet in Britain and India

Britain Average daily consumption 3150 calories

India Average daily consumption 1800 calories

cereals (carbohydrates)

other carbohydrates

meat and fish proteins

milk and eggs

fresh fruit and vegetables (vitamins)

other proteins

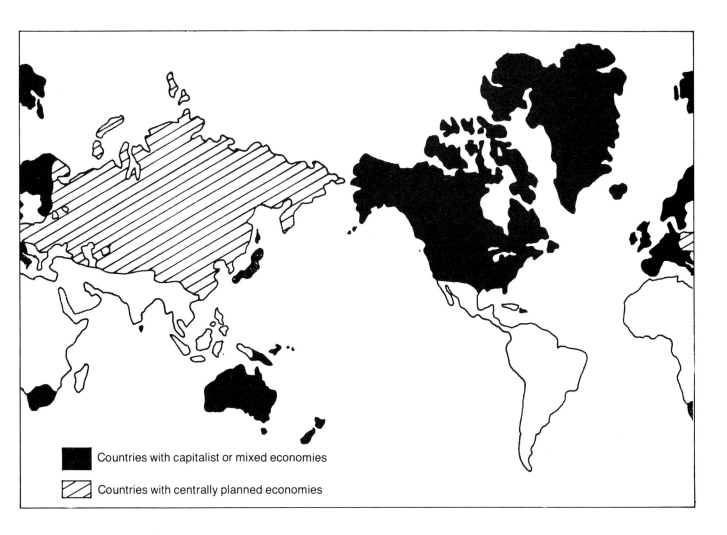

Countries with capitalist or mixed economies

Countries with centrally planned economies

17. A divided world

Although we are all members of the human race, we live in a very divided world. There are differences in hereditary, environment, culture, tradition, values, religion, politics, race, social conditions.

Differences exist between black and white; between those who live in town and countryside; between rich and poor. One of the things dividing the world is the different systems of government and different economic systems.''

Britain and most other countries of the western world have democratic governments and forms of capitalism with private ownership. The People's Republic of China, the Soviet Union and many other countries; believe in communism; this means production being owned by the state.

In between there is a Third World of developing countries but there is wide spread poverty. A large number of people in these countries are suffering from starvation.

J. Nobbs 'Introducing Social Studies'

(a) Name one country other than that stated in the text that is a Capitalist Country.

(b) Name one country other than those stated in the text that is a Communist Country.

(c) Name one country that can be described as a developing country.

State why you think "A large number of the people in these countries are suffering from starvation".

What steps can be taken to deal with the problem of the poor nations.

The aim of the United Nations has been to promote understanding between nations. From your Social Studies work state whether you think they will be successful (if not Why?)

Index